Tempus ORAL HISTORY *Series*

Buckingham
voices

Gas explosion in Bridge Street around 1960 - so much for High Speed Gas! (J.G.)

Tempus ORAL HISTORY *Series*

Buckingham
voices

Compiled by
Robert Cook
with
Des Tunks

TEMPUS

Tempus Publishing Limited
The Mill, Brimscombe Port,
Stroud, Gloucestershire, GL5 2QG

ISBN 0 7524 2198 0

Typesetting and origination by
Tempus Publishing Limited
Printed in Great Britain by
Midway Colour Print, Wiltshire

Acknowledgements

We are grateful to all who have contributed photographs and anecdotes. Everyone mentioned in this book has made great efforts to assist and advise. They have shared the benefit of their wisdom and experience. We hope to have done them justice.

Special thanks are due to Henry and Esme Thomas for help and encouragement behind the scenes, Clive Birch MBE, Joe Pallett, Phillips & Sons, John Ganderton and the *Buckingham and Winslow Advertiser*. Photographs are from the collections of the compilers except where indicated by the initials of the following people who kindly made them available:

Muriel Adkins (M.A.); *Buckingham and Winslow Advertiser* (B.W.A.); Clive Birch (C.B.); Pip Brimson (P.B.), H.C. Casserley (H.C.C.), R.M. Casserley (R.M.C.), Harry Claridge (H.C.), R.H. Chapman (R.H.C.), John Credland (J.C.), Grace Durham (G.D.), John Ganderton (J.G.), Ed Grimsdale (E.G.), the late Gwen Harris (G.H.), Initial Photographics/Colin Stacey (I.P.), Joyce Stern (J.S.), Derek Knibbs (D.K.), Frank R. Markham (F.R.M.), Chris Phillips (C.P.), Dandy Robinson (D.R.), Andrew Shouler (A.S.), Bill Tomkins (B.T.), Frank Taylor (F.T.), Mrs Nora Twelvetrees (N.T.), Gillian Wain (G.W.), Sheila Stern (S.S.).

Contents

Introduction

Local history can arouse great passions which may be surprising in a world made smaller through modern technology and rapid transport. This could be because the world has become less personal and people have become more possessive of their own backyards which are increasingly threatened by the pace of modern development. Open spaces are fewer and the highway less a road to freedom than somewhere to join a traffic jam on the way to work, supermarket or holiday.

Buckingham, like most of the south east, suffers from its own success. Legendary local newsman Vic Tattershall reported in 1971 that Alderman Tom Lambourne may have lit the blue touch paper on the town's housing debate. Failure to provide homes for a key council workman had highlighted shortages, he said. With proposed population expansion up to 18,000 and expected location of the Independent University of Buckingham, more public service workers would need accommodation and letting them queue jump would cause trouble, it was argued. At the time, the town's three largest industrialists were clamouring for more council housing.

By May 1995 the *Buckingham Advertiser* reported that the town's young faced a homeless crisis because of the shortage of affordable accommodation and lawless behaviour of certain youthful elements had become an ongoing issue. Vivien McMellon noted, in the same newspaper, that it was becoming unfashionable to dissent from the popular views of the permissive society. She suggested that if parents did not make a stand children would have no basis upon which to develop a sense of morality. Ladies who had been at the Royal Latin School during the Swinging Sixties lamented the girls' rising hem lines while gentlemen observed that with so many girls favouring trousers now you can't tell them from the boys!

Fashion is, of course, everything now and the youth market is huge. Mobile phones are commonplace around town, a must have fashion accessory and people walk or almost drive into you as they are so busy using them. Who is to argue? People get their views and opinions from farther afield now, not from the vicar or terrifying school master. More often it's the teacher who's terrified of the pupils and doesn't want to go to school!

Schools struggle to keep pace with the town's expansion while politicians and planning officials announce that expanding Milton Keynes is good for Buckingham – making land and executive housing even more desirable – and expensive. House prices have increased by 135% in real terms since 1970 and wages by only 60% (National Housing Federation and the

Chartered Institute of Housing report). So the woman of the house has to work whether she wants to be liberated or not!

At least Buckingham has a Vision Design statement which makes certain safeguards against some of the more philistine designs of the last 20 years but that does nothing to cut costs The government are looking for over 3 million new houses in the south east by 2016, threatening 39 square kilometres in Bucks. Local countryside is going to change even more.

But without change people would still be shivering through long winters down by Bucca's original settlement on a bend in the River Ouse. There have always been voices for and against the changes, some see profit, others loss. Some voices have greater powers of amplification – so much so that some will say nothing on the 'big issues' but have much to say on the day-to-day pleasures and problems. They are all voices and all worth listening to; weaving a tapestry of an ever changing scene.

Robert Cook and Desmond Tunks (December 2000)

Town Hall and Market Square, c. 1912.

Family group, early 1900s. (D.K.)

CHAPTER 1
Breathing Space

Castle Street, early 1930s. Buckingham was a child of war, a Saxon stronghold against the Danelaw and briefly the centre of military, civil and administrative society. It acquired an overwhelming overlord, made little progress, and its significance slowly leached away through geography, politics and lack of motivation and while its position on relatively level ground made it accessible, it was at the wrong end of the county, in a sort of economic 'no man's land'. For centuries the town served an agricultural hinterland, then in the last century it was dramatically affected by the transport revolution, somewhat later than other such towns. (Clive Birch MBE)

Little Shop

I was born in 1909. I first remember living at Steeple Claydon. Me dad was killed working on the railway at Neasden in 1918. Our family was four boys and me

mother and all we got was £3 a month pension from the railway. I can't think how she coped. She set up a little shop. Some days she used to say I don't want you to go to school this afternoon. We used to walk from Steeple Claydon across the

A Knibbs family wedding, early twentieth century. (D.K.)

fields at Hillesden, with a basket each. We'd go round Hillesden with these little bits. Called at the school with a pennorth o' sweets in a little bag; kids used to come out. That's how we survived.

Stan Beckett

Daddy

I was born in 1912 at Willesden. Old grampy fetched me out to watch a Zeppelin come down at Potters Bar. Those days it was all hills. I remember playing matches in the street when the little Gotha bombers came over. Mother worked in a munitions factory and came home yellow as hell. Dad was in the army.

I remember mother kept saying, 'Go out and wait till your dad comes home.' I went up to every soldier calling him 'daddy'. I didn't know what dad looked like.

Grampy

Grampy was a builder. When he retired he took the Crown Pub at the bottom of the hill in Gawcott. There were stables for horses and a lovely orchard at the back. We used to play a game swinging a horse shoe. That was in the 1920s when the Prince of Wales and his brother used to come here for fox hunting with the Bicester hounds. They came to the Crown to stable their horses and had a room to change in.

Playing the fiddle

One time when the hunt was meeting at Hillesden, this old boy, I think he was a Buckland, was playing his fiddle and the Prince of Wales gave him a gold sovereign. His widow kept it in a frame years after.

Royal Visit

The princes came one day. One became Edward VIII until he went off with Mrs Simpson and the other became George VI. He used to stutter a bit. They came in the pub with their equerry and ordered three glasses of White Horse whiskey. The old gramp gave it to them and they went upstairs to their room. Soon after the equerry came back saying; 'This isn't *White Horse!*' The old gramp said, 'I know, it's Black and White and if you lot up there can't drink it you know what you can do; bugger off.' We did laugh. they done no more but got up and went and never came back anymore. Gramp wouldn't have any nonsense whether they were king or what.

Bill Tomkins

Got a Bike

I came from Hillesden. There was nothing else to do except the brickyard. My dad was a farm worker. You had to get a job of some kind. It was hard work but you had to put up with it. Before I was married I lived at Twyford so it was only two miles to walk. In 1932 I got married and moved to Hillesden. Then I got a push bike. We didn't get the buses till after the war. Blokes biked long distances: Bicester, Brill, Akeley, Syresham, a long ride before and after a days work.

Arthur Chilton

Trousers Down

We had an old Welshman teaching us at Twyford. He was a devil. I've seen him fetch old boys out in the porch, let their trousers down, whack 'em anyhow. Well this particular morning it was Ascension Day. There was a boy sat with me on the forms and he couldn't do his sums. Arithmetic was one of my pet subjects and I was showing another boy how to do something. Old Parry spotted us, and stopped the class. I weren't taking notice of what he was doing on the board. When he asked me I couldn't answer. He got both of us by the backs of our necks, dragged us out, gave us a shove. There was a frame with bits of chalk in used for drawing the five lines for music onto the blackboard. In my paddy as he hit me, I pushed this thing, sending it flying. Cor he gave me such a clout. Then off he marched us all, two by two, to Ascension Day service at the church. Next morning it was all forgotten.

Can You Play?

I played for Claydon Boys at football, then when we came to Twyford I had to play against them. The April I left school I was playing football with the men. I used to stand outside the old shop on Saturday morning waiting for the brick workers to come home, hoping and praying the secretary would say they were one short and 'Can you play?' I used to ride to the

Buckingham Parish Church looking very Dickensian with so much snow. Religion once ruled the public face of local life.

game on the crossbar of a bloke's bike.

She'd Say No!

The schoolmaster came up to me just before I left school. He said, 'Stanley can you ask your mother if you can play football in the final at Buckingham with the men on Saturday. That was Tuesday. I knew she'd say no. So I went up the road for a few minutes, went back to the school and said, 'Yes Sir, I can play.' I was just coming up to fourteen. I was at Ford Meadow in 1924. They'd been playing there since the nineteenth century. It was a big thing. I've seen 'em three and four deep.

Stan Beckett

Anti-Sport

I was very anti-sport. I didn't like it at school when they said, 'You will turn up on Saturday afternoon for a rugger match.' It was purgatory. When I left school I promised myself I'd never go to a football or rugger match and I didn't.

Frank Markham

We All Played Together

I was born in North End Square in 1917. As I grew up everybody knew everybody else. That was it. Children all played together. There was a little shop and an alley led up to more houses where my grandmother lived. That's where the old peoples' flats are now.

Mrs Woodfield

Come Next Spring

Mother remarried in 1921 and we moved to Twyford. I've been here ever since. times were damned hard. We had to do all sorts of jobs, had what we called the 'Saturday penny' for doing all manner of things about the house. At fourteen I left school and went to work for Colonel Fitzgerald in the gardens of Twyford Manor. I started at 5 a.m. working until 5 p.m. in the week and noon on Saturday when this lady used to come out with a brand new ten-bob note, old red one. Out of that I used to give me mother five shilling. I went down to the shop which used to sell bikes. Used to pay the shopkeeper half a crown a week till I'd paid for it. That was my pocket money to get what I wanted. In the autumn Lord Chesham took over the manor as a hunting box. He was master of the hunt. They got me to work indoors then. Still on ten bob, but being fed. Come next Spring he bought the place and it had to be renovated. They all cleared out back to Latimer and I went back into the garden which suited me because I could play cricket out there.

Stan Beckett

Local schoolboys' enthusiasm for football is as strong as ever in this Steeple Claydon scene, April 1997.

Buckingham Town Football Team early 1920s.(D.T.)

When George Went to Work

The late George Jenkins told me how he started working for Phillips and Sons in January 1922. The showroom was the front half of the present building and held three vehicles. His first job at 7 a.m. was sweeping the blue brick path outside. Working hours were 7 a.m. to 8 a.m., breakfast and on to 1 p.m. for dinner until 2 p.m. There were no ten-minute tea breaks. There was a hand operated lift, made up of a platform, four upright beams, pulleys, cables and a winch in the yard to raise carts and carriages up to the first floor above the showroom; which was the paint shop. In later years small cars or car bodies that had been removed from their chassis were also hauled up for painting by the experts. Most paint was in

powdered form requiring grinding or milling and mixing with oil. Then it was painted onto the shop wall to test for consistency, causing a paint build up inches thick over the years. When George went to work there as a youngster he encountered the firm's seventy-year-old blacksmith, Mr Rawlings, who walked over 4 miles each way to work. He remembered how cold it could be working out in the yard bays removing axles, road springs etc. Next to these bays was the 'Battery house' where a Blackstone oil engine drove a direct current dynamo and supplied lighting for the whole company. The bottom garage opened onto Ford Street, prone to flooding whenever the River Ouse bursts its banks, as it did most winters, often with the water rising over 4ft. There was room for two cars inside the garage and old

Fleece Yard 1935,. (P.B.)

W.K. Knibbs, haulage contractor poses with perhaps a 'shy' Mrs Knibbs! Their son is peeping through the window.

Billy Baughan, 'Tecky' had a small room above where he mended punctures, carrying the heavy tyres and wheels up a small wooden staircase. A new 'Stenor' electronic vulcanising machine enabled him to repair previously unrepairable tyres.

Joe Pallett

round with the old grandfather helping him shepherd the animals down by the osier beds. There used to be an old ram down there, I went with grandfather to 'start him up'. There used to be Greyhound racing over at Westfields. Uncle Fred had some field glasses. We saw the old airship, R101, go over in the 1930s.

Des Tunks

The Fields Around

The Big Ground out toward Gawcott Road was our playground. They put the wireless station up there when the war started. I remember the time we went

Best Of It

I enjoyed my times with Swan Wheelers before the war. We had the best of it.

Quiet roads and tea runs. All very sociable it was then. There weren't many ladies among us, which was perhaps a pity. I had a semi-racing bike. On tour we averaged about 15 m.p.h.

Martin Blane

Man From Dunlop

My grandfather William was a member of Swan Wheelers. He made bicycles himself, when the family garage business was on the opposite side of the road. He bought steel tubes to make the frames in his small workshop. The man from Dunlop came by train from Birmingham to sell him tyres and tubes. William

Morris at Oxford was his next call after grandad. Our business started in June 1849 as A.W. Ganderton, Wheelwrights and Agricultural Engineers.

John Ganderton

Stones In Good Order

We left Waddesdon when I was nine, the tenant at Thornborough Mill, Harry Dormer, having died. The mill had already been put in my father's name sometime before. It was decided my father and mother should go there. We were a milling family. My grandfather had a big family, eleven in all. We had a miller at Thornborough, his name was John

Phillip's Garage early 1900s, (C.P.)

Morton. He was an awkward old man. A miller's work was to keep the stones in good order and make sure the meal was of good quality. The stones had to be dressed from time to time, depending on how much they were used. The top stone is called the runner and the bottom one the bed stone. The top one gets most wear so you take out the bed stone which was originally a runner, replace it with the runner and put a new stone as runner. The corn went up in sacks on a hoist. You fastened a chain round the neck of the sack. you needed someone at the top. My wife helped me sometimes. In the summer, the miller normally helped out on the land. We had 45 acres with the mill.

Frank Taylor

Cream Was Good

I went to work at the Milk factory when it was owned by Thew, Hooker and Gilby. The site in Chandos Road was close to the railway and trucks of dairy products were backed in, loaded and unloaded daily. Wilts United Dairies took it over in the 1920s and the business expanded. There were garages and repair shops for the lorries. A huge tank was built for condensing milk. I earned 6s extra cleaning it. It was very hot inside. We made all sorts of things there and our cream was good enough for me to make regular trips to Buckingham Palace. In those days cream cost 2s 6d a gallon and farmers earned 11d a gallon for their milk.

Bill Tomkins

Bullnose

I was born in Bournemouth where father had a boarding house. My grandfather had started the ironmongers business in the Market Square in 1875. I went to Miss Dentchfield's kindergarten school in Chandos Road for a year or two. There were about fifteen pupils. Then I went to Gawcott Council School. We moved to Bedford when I was eight. Father retired and in a short space of time grandfather died and the business passed to his son-in-law Cyril Charles Evenson who had married my Aunt Flo. Around 1904 the business moved to larger premises by the White Hart. These had been built in 1850 and were a shoe factory for a long time. My Uncle Charles Evenson, who had been a buyer for a builder's merchants, eventually went blind. I remember early days when he had a 1926 Bullnose Morris. I thought it was marvellous going along at 28 mph!

Frank Markham

Two Lamb Chops

I remember the housekeeper at Stowe School, where I delivered the meat when I worked at the old butchers. I used to go out on the old bike with the basket at the front. Biked all the way up to Stowe school. They'd ring up. Never called you by your Christian name. 'Woodfield you'd better get on your bike and go and take Mrs Hannaway two lamb chops.' So of I'd ride, right up to the school with two chops in the basket. Old Reggie Spencer used to open his old sweet shop, Sunday night in North End Square. He'd say 'What do you bloody well want? Well I 'ent got them buggers now.' He used to swear at us. He had an off licence too.

Bob Tyzack of Preston Bissett lorry driver extraordinaire in 1992.

Fat Old Boy

You were frightened of the police. They used to ride about in a motor bike and sidecar. One of them was old Darville at Tingewick, a big fat old boy. He had a push bike. Darville was a good old boy. He used to come on my bus in the 1930s. He was a Newport Pagnell bloke really. They used to get off at Stony Stratford and catch another bus to Newport. I knew he'd come back the same day. He'd look out for me in Stony and say, 'Come on, have a beer.' They drove buses and had a beer in those days.

Bert Woodfield

Bellring

We used to open Reggie Spencer's shop door on purpose just to hear the bell ring. There was always a comic and a gang of boys standing round telling jokes Sunday nights.

Des Tunks

Violent With The Drink

Some were violent with the drink, others just daft. Tommy Jones came down the Brittania one Christmas and drank a bit. He said to Bert Clark, 'You coming down home for a drink then Bert?' He said, 'yes'.

Girl relaxing by the old mill stream Thornborough. (F.T.)

His wife had been making Christmas puddings and he put one on top of the Christmas tree, tipping it over. She swore at him like anything. Billy Dillow used to go home sozzled to Gawcott Road, when I was a kid. He pulled the mantelpiece down once and threw it in the road. He weren't like that when he was in the pub. His father had got like elephants feet and they used to tie the horse to a pole on the corner. There was always characters. But people were mainly more honest then. They were all in the same boat, not out to cut each other's throats or get one another down so to speak. They shared what they could grow on their allotments. The majority of older people were church or chapel going.

Des Tunks

Not A Dirty Man

Alf Varney always looked black, as if he'd been under a lorry, oil on him, all his trousers creased. He always had his shave at Jim Boot's. I was in there one day. He was having a shave and this kid was in there and he said, 'The dustman is having a hair cut'. Jim was annoyed because it was embarrassing. Bill Boots said, 'Oh no, he's just been round cleaning buses, he's not a dirty man.' There was always characters in the pubs, but there was rarely trouble. Maybe there'd be a few scuffles at a dance but it would be one on one, not like today, a dozen on one.

Bert Woodfield

Poor Old Chap

Every Tuesday gramps used to take his white pony and cart down to Buckingham from Gawcott and get blind drunk. It was the pony that found the way back, not him, poor old chap. They just put him on the cart; the pony found his own way back into the stable.

Bill Tomkins

Little Man

Our family came here from near Banbury when dad went to work on the estate at Maids Moreton. I remember on the old Canon Corner they always had the old RAC man standing there from nine o'clock in the morning until half past five at night. Little man, his name was Watts. Them days it was only bicycles and horses and carts. Now there's all this traffic and there's no one there! He only lived near the church. If you done something wrong he'd shout and tell you off.

Joe Pallett

'Toodling Around'

I passed my heavy goods test on an Albion chain drive with solid tyres and paraffin side lights, when I was eighteen Old chain drive lorries made hell of a noise and oil used to collect in a can by the engine. When it was full I used to stop and empty it on the chain. I had to know about engines. If anything went wrong with your lorry you'd stay with the fitter while they showed you how to fix it. I enjoyed 'toodling' around the lanes collecting milk churns with my lorry. One churn held 10 gallons and I checked the measure. I once worked 34 hours without a break. Hit the milk factory gate because oil had leaked onto the hub so the brakes slipped. So I was given an 8 gallon drum to keep topping it up for the night run to London. Manager said, 'If you don't make it you're sacked!' It was lovely driving through the countryside and its green fields. Roads were half the size and if you met a horse and cart you had to get up on the grass. Towns were small and traffic scarce. It was surprising how quickly we got to places. In my early days I was brake man in charge of a trailer. Often I'd have to guide my driver through thick London fog walking in front following the tram lines with my torch. Lorry only had paraffin sidelights and no wipers. Had to have half the windscreen open to hand wipe the other side. One day we were crawling through fog when a woman came running up to the cab shouting 'Help my car's on fire!' I got down and had a look and it was just the fog. My happiest day was when I rounded a bend to pull into a farm and saw a lovely girl emptying a bucket in the hedge and going back to fill another. She was in service and they used to send her to the village pump. I think she was waiting for me, she did smile as I came along and she was working that old pump. We saw each other every day after that and got married when she was twenty-one. They were happy days.

Bill Tomkins

Horse and Trap on Gawcott Road, c. 1900. (D.K.)

Best of rivals: Damon Hill and Michael Schumacher at a post British Grand Prix press conference, 1994. Damon won and Michael's expression speaks for itself. (B.W.A.)

He Could Play Piano

Bert Tomkins lived next to the Grand Junction pub. He had two sons, Bert and Peter. Bert had his Metro Dance Band. Proper character, he liked his drink and women. Became caretaker at the senior school. He got on very well with women because he could play a piano. People came in the pub with requests. Proper entertainer he was. He was a lot older than me, but I went round with him up until the war started. He had a BSA three wheeler. We'd go to dances at Brackley and he'd get sozzled. First weekend after I joined up he went off with old Jack Kelly and tipped it over. That was it, finished his playing. Jack had a scar right down his face and they weren't friends after that. I went into the RAF.

Bert Woodfield

Stop Whistling

When old Bodenham was headmaster at the senior school he said, 'Tomkins, I've told you before about that whistling.' But old Bill couldn't help it. He was caretaker and when they'd all gone home he'd have half an hour on the piano in the hall. His wife was a good darts player. I used to partner her playing in the Grand Junction and the Horse and Groom. The senior school was built in 1935 and I went up in 1936. They did away with gardening classes. Sadly, because they were a great help to kids leaving school. They had chickens and pigs which wasn't new to me because we bred our own pigs.

Des Tunks

Bert Tomkin's Leyland Milk Truck and trailer at the Milk Factory in Chandos Road. He started as brake man controlling the trailer. (B.T.)

Smelt Different

We came to Buckingham in February 1938. My father got a job with Hillier & Son as a printer and bookbinder. He was in his sixties when he was made redundant at Ipswich. He found an enormous flat over a fancy goods shop in Buckingham Market Square. I liked it because it was different, and it smelt different; a peculiar smell, fascinating. It was just oldness. There were funny old cupboards all over the place. The staircase down to the shop was boarded up. There was no bathroom but we finally got one of the big rooms at the back converted. We rented

James Robert Tunks at the Milk Factory Pig Farm. The dairy fed skimmed the milk and fed waste to the pigs as a sideline.

from a curious old chap called Reggie Spencer. I didn't like him much. The kitchen was very large, approached by stairs from the passage behind the shops. It was draughty until we got the porch. We had to cart the hot water upstairs to a washstand but for all its faults it was nice to have this outlook over the market square, you could see everything that was going on through very big windows. There was no very heavy traffic.

Pip Brimson (née Beck)

A Dirty Job

I drove the Bedford Blue coaches. They ran a service, Bedford to Oxford, twice daily, out at 9 a.m to Oxford, back to Buckingham at 12 noon, then to Bedford. They'd be back in Buckingham at 4 p.m. They also had this small coach which I drove. I kept it up where the old launderette was in Tingewick Road. Tubby Hitchcock had a garage there. They used to keep a Shell petrol tanker in there as well. We did a few odd jobs in the district picking up people like Chandos Bowls Club or Wilts United Dairies Social trips. Mr Gammon owned the business and his daughter collected fares on the Oxford-Bedford run. I was only earning just over £2 a week just before the war, June 1939. I told Mr Gammon I was going to drive for the London Brick Company at Calvert. 'A dirty job', he said. I said, 'I know, but it's clean money.'

Bert Woodfield

Build A Cinema

Father had run a cinema near Stratford on Avon. That gave him the idea. He promised my mother he'd build a cinema with a house beside it and he did; at the junction of Chandos Road and London Road. Before that people watched silent films in the Town Hall where Mrs Webb played piano, slowing and accelerating her music according to the drama on screen.

Gwen Harris (née Parker)

Cowboys!

When I was very young I went to see the *Cross-Eyed Cowboy*, a film at the Town Hall. The last time I walked in there with my tuppence there was no one there to collect the ticket so I sat down in the front row!

Bert Woodfield

Well Built

I worked for Meadows drapers after school. When Mr Meadows put the sales on, the best price Balito stockings were 11 ¾d that was in 1938. He wrote out the price. 'That'll do,' he said. I was there until I was thirteen, on 3 shillings a week. I was only cleaner and errand boy. Edie Cecil was manageress. She was plump and well built and nice looking. She used to give me her money to put in the post office savings every week. She liked to try the latest things on. Every Saturday morning she'd shout down from upstairs 'Desmond, have you

Chandos Cinema, late 1940s, and only one car in sight – how different today! (G.H.)

The bakery, September 1998: a tradition survives.

polished the brass? Have you finished?' She said, 'You must say 'Yes Mr Meadows, No Mr Meadows.' Meadows' shop was smothered in mice. This bloke shouted, 'Mouse there, mouse there!' and told me to put my foot on it. Mr Meadows was very smart, over six foot, dressed in a black suit, hair parted on one side. His wife wasn't much over five foot, smart, slim, with long hair hanging down her back. I went to work at the bakery, that was hard. Mostly cleaning in the cookhouse, delivering cakes to Stowe School, you could get soaked cycling all that way in the rain. I used to scrub the alleyway. I cooked the doughnuts, putting the jam in. It was hard work for 1s 6d a week.

Des Tunks

Crash

I remember a plane force landing on the estate where dad worked at Lillingstone Dayrell. I was nine or ten, turned out he was distantly related to the Robarts who's land he'd crashed on.

Out Of Court

I was born $4\frac{1}{2}$ miles from Buckingham and it was our local town, delivery vans coming out with most things we needed. we had to go to Buckingham for shoe repairs, chemist etc. We relied on our bicycles. In the 1930s cars were parked each side of the market square, right outside W.H. Smiths on Tuesday and

Saturday when the market was on. One day Captain Robarts was passing the market stalls when he caught his bumper on a trestle table of crockery; cups saucers were strewn as far as the old post office. I think the settlement was out of court! On Saturday evening the Salvation Army always played in the Bull Ring. George Smith was the bandmaster. It was a very good band, whether you were a Salvationist or not you enjoyed it. It was a big loss when they got rid of the village length man, he kept the gutters clear and sanded the black spots in the winter, just with a shovel, no spreaders. Generally I think people helped each other a lot more. When we cycled to school we had no fear of needing any help. No matter which house you knocked at somebody would help you.

Such A Joy

Coming to Buckingham was such a joy in the late 1930s. I began to look around the countryside. We'd moved around a lot when I was a child but this was gorgeous. I used to walk a lot. I never minded walking on my own. I was about sixteen, I used to cycle as well; miles and miles. I'd won a scholarship to my school in Ipswich and could have gone to the Royal Latin School but I'd been to twelve different schools in ten years and what with the expenses for uniform etc., I told my mother I wanted to get a job instead. I worked at the bakery, which I didn't like, but I liked Miss Doris Rolfe who ran the shop. She was kind but I didn't like Mrs Coulson who owned it. She was overbearing. It had its interesting side. I was asked to go downstairs and help in the

Pip Beck, third from right, standing with drama/musical group, c.1938. (P.B.)

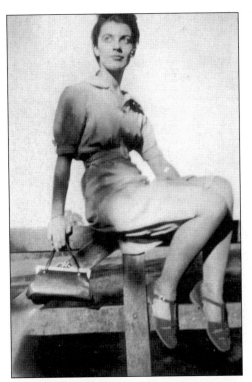

Pip Brimson (née Beck) enjoying the freedom and fresh air off Stowe Avenue, c.1938. (P.B.)

restaurant. The farmers used to come in for the Tuesday luncheon when the cattle markets were on. They had a special price. Doris showed me what to do. I got a few tips which I was ambivalent about accepting, but I thought, 'Oh well, it's a little bit more!' That went on for three months, then I saw outside Lesley's the hairdressers, a notice board advertising for an apprentice to learn hairdressing and beauty culture. I liked the sound of it and was accepted. Only snag was they required a premium. My mother had a chat and it was agreed I could go without a premium but receive no wages. I enjoyed some of the work, but there was a lot of basin cleaning, sweeping up hair and polishing the floor in the passageway. Mr Lesley and

his sister Nora did the chiropody in a room upstairs and keeping the room tidy became my job too. My mother objected because they weren't teaching me while I did this and she said I should ask for wages. I said, 'I can't', but I did. They refused at first, but then I got 9 shillings a week.

Silk Stockings

I spent my wages on things like silk stockings. There weren't any nylons. They cost about 2s a pair. I gave 2s to my mother and bought a little make up. Mother wouldn't let me use too much. She'd say 'You don't want that muck on your face!'

Frightfully Expensive

I used to look at the cosmetics that Moira used for the beauty counter at Lesley's and thought, 'Oh I'd like to use those.' They were in turquoise, enamel containers with brass tops and looked frightfully expensive.

Church Lady

There was a girls' club run by Miss Williams, a church lady who worked as a cashier at W.H. Smiths. I helped her. I met some nice girls. We did all sorts of things. We sang songs around the piano and danced. One of the older girls worked in Hillier's and knew my father. She taught me to dance. We played darts. It was quite a good evening for us.

Rememberance Weekend, 1998. The white house in the background is up for restoration, but tradition is the theme here in the square. (R.J.C.)

Lion's Cage

I went to other socials. Some were run by big firms like Wilts United Dairies. They got you into knowing people. You progressed to Saturday night dances, somebody like Bill Boots and the New Blue Orpheans played the music. His father Jimmy was the barber. Bill told me that when his father was a young man he was the first to go into a Lion's cage when the circus came to Buckingham.

Big Ball

The upper level of the town hall was practically all dance hall. Nobody got very drunk at Saturday night dances. There were plenty of local pubs for that. Modern dances look awful by comparison, all those horrible lasers and flashing lights. We used to have a big ball suspended from the ceiling. As it rotated you got light reflected off it, making rainbow speckles all over everybody.

Drugs

I'd never heard of drugs then. My parents never cautioned me about drink, but I wouldn't have dared to come home having drunk alcohol, though when I was sixteen or seventeen, I had the odd gin and lime.

Dress

People dressed up at the more expensive events, like the police or hunt balls. The Hunt Ball was the classy one. I had a couple of evening dresses which were made for me by my mother and I felt really glamorous in them. One was bright organdie. It wasn't new. It was given to my mother who was good at sewing and altering things to fit me. A friend gave me another one which looked nice, made of a fine material, sort of transparent, brown with a satin fitted slip underneath in the same colour, with long sleeves. I made a little Juliet cap with gold sequins to go with it. Another dress, for ordinary dances, was deep blue with an enormously full skirt, not very long. When I twirled round the skirt was flung out all around me. I thought it was great. I went out and bought a lot of fancy binding, it was very pretty in two colours; a lighter blue and orchid pink. I put three bands around the body, a band around the neck and short sleeves. I adored that dress, I felt so good in it.

Pip Brimson (née Beck)

Local girls relax in the sunshine off Stowe Avenue, this was 1938 and the calm before the storm. (P.B)

CHAPTER 2
Armed and Dangerous

Britain faced war poorly prepared in 1939, having refused to face facts as a nation. In November 1939, it was recommended to Buckingham Borough Council that the old German gun placed in front of the Old Gaol be offered to the government for any purpose for which it might be useful. But the nation really needed fit young men and here are some of Buckingham & District's finest ready for departure from the Market Square, 1939. (P.B.)

Home Guard Entertainment

All the above are extracts from the Home Guard Social Club Minute Book recorded by Bert Williams and supplied by his daughter Joy Stern.

There was a concert put on in the Town Hall on 22 December 1940. The price of admission for Buckingham Platoon Home Guard members and Buckingham Town service men was ls 6d, other Home Guard and service men 2s 0d. No service women allowed. I agreed to ask Mrs Hocking to

The CHANDOS CINEMA

(BUCKINGHAM) LTD.

Managing Director: E. PARKER   Telephone: Buckingham 3196

Monday, February 12th   **For Three Days**

ERROL FLYNN in
Uncertain Glory
(A Cert.)

SHORTS
NEWS

Monday at 5.30 and 8
Tuesday and Wednesday at 7.30

Thursday, February 15th   **For Three Days**

RAY MILLAND and GINGER ROGERS in
Lady In The Dark
(U Cert.)

SHORTS
NEWS

Friday 7.30
Thursday and Saturday 5.30 and 8

Same film for Children Saturday Matinee at 2.15 p.m.

Babies in arms and small children not admitted to evening performances

---

Tonight—20 MILLION SWEETHEARTS (U Cert.)

PRICES OF ADMISSION

EVENING: Stalls 9d., 1/- and 1/9; Balcony 2/3
Children (accompanied by parent) Stalls 1/-, 9d., Balcony 1/6
Advance Booking: Balcony 2/6; Back Stalls 2/-

CHILDREN'S MATINEE SATURDAY:
Under 14: Stalls 4d.; Balcony 9d.
Adults: Stalls 1/-; Balcony 1/9

No reduced prices for children on Saturday Evenings.

Booking Office Open 10—12 a.m.

The booking office will be closed on Wednesday mornings until further notice

Children will not be admitted to " A " films unless accompanied by parent or guardian.

Chandos Cinema advertisements in February 1945. (B.W.A.)

provide the entertainment up to the sum of £7. It was agreed to ask Mr Mowat to provide the beer and to ask all attending to bring their own mugs or glasses and plates.

Smoking Concert

It was decided to invite the following to the Smoking Concert; six members of the fire brigade, Mr Osborne, Webb, Seaton, Dolman, Allitt, Bower, Wright, Rant, Col Gregson, Slack, Taylor and Vyle. It was agreed to allow Ms Williams up to £5 for refreshments for the smoking concert. It was agreed to allow each member at the smoking concert half a pint of beer each, also to get 200 cigarettes Mr Barr gave permission to all members to attend in uniform.

Proposed by Mr Jones, secretary that a letter of thanks be sent to the judges of the flower show.

It was decided to hold a Whist drive for members of the Sports Club and their friends, each member to be allowed to bring two friends, the price to be 1s 6d for the three and the prizes to be vouchers to the value of 5s, 3s 6d, and 2s 6d and that we give refreshments. After a long discussion about the Red Cross effort it was decided to wait and see if we could get the town hall before we do any more.

It was decided to give a tea to club members, their wives and children and also run other competitions, the tea to be free and no charge be made to enter any of the events for sports or classes for the flower show.

After hearing that the British Legion were leaving their club room, and they would not be able to let us have it during the winter months as in the previous winter. Mr Williams announced that we had got the offer to use the Church End club room. It was decided to accept this offer if we could not get another room. At a later discussion Mr Jones announced that the British Legion had been granted an extension for the use of their room It was decided to ask them for the use of it on Friday nights on the same terms as last year. Mr Williams proposed that we send all our ex-members serving abroad, 200 cigarettes and also send Sgt Cummings the same.

It was agreed to invite the mothers and smaller children and also any evacuees staying with them, to the concert in the evening. The date, place, and other arrangements were left until a later meeting.

Last Season

It was proposed by Mr Butler, seconded by Mr Wheeler that we give the Buckingham Cricket Club a donation of £2 2s 0d for the use of their ground and kit last season.

Roughest Of Rough

When war started there was a Pioneer Corps army camp at Tingewick. They were the roughest of the rough. I dreaded them coming in. There were a few drunks you had to get rid of. That was the time when films came by train from Bletchley and we'd only got one reel of this particularly important film. I had to announce to the audience that they must be patient while my husband rushed to Bletchley for the other reel. I took over running the cinema in 1941 when my father died.

Gwen Harris (née Parker)

Relief

People didn't understand what the Pioneer Corps were doing. Jobs like handling ammunition was a hard and dirty job. Obviously sometimes they might look a bit rough if anyone saw them working. Most of the ones at Tingewick weren't A1 grade. I was in the Pioneer Corps and would have gone to Japan if the Americans hadn't dropped the nuclear bomb on Hiroshima. The men went crazy with relief. But I enjoyed my army service. I got really fit. We were like all British servicemen, badly paid compared to the Americans. The Americans, though, were always generous and friendly in my experience.

Des Tunks

No Profit

Colonel Harris at Thornton Hall used to have a barge load of coal at a time, so he came to my father one day to start a coal business up again because the barges had ceased. Father reluctantly agreed. The coal was unloaded at Thornton Hall and that went on right through the war, but there was no profit in it. The cheapest coal was 1s 11d a hundredweight, the best was 2s 3d. We unloaded the coal at Lechamstead Wharf. It was hard work. We packed up after the war.

Frank Taylor

Pretty Fit!

When I was sixteen and a half I had to join the Home Guard. I'd get home from Calvert brick works at six and have to be on parade by half past. You had to explain why you were late. If the sirens went at midnight you'd be called out to protect the town. You might have to run three miles to the Lone Tree Inn or to Tingewick. You ran with your section. No telling when you'd get to bed and you'd still have to get up for work! Still I found the energy to play football at lunch time. I was pretty fit.

Des Tunks

The Old Hen!

I was due to start at the Royal Latin School in September 1939. Because of the war some masters had volunteered and they needed more teachers so there was a delay. I think H.B. Toft was head when I started, but I only remember Dr Foster, a plump man. The headmistress was Miss Merry, an inappropriate name considering that she was strict, fierce, tall and thin. We called her 'the old hen'.

They all wore caps and gowns then. Maths was my favourite subject, taught by Mr Allett, a really nice man. I lived at Mursley. They supplied me with a bicycle to get to Swanbourne station. Then I travelled to Buckingham via Verney Junction. We walked from the station down Chandos Road, passed the milk factory with all its old smoke and steam gushing everywhere, to school. There'd be lorries loading and unloading. They kept pigs down near the Mitre pub, which they fattened on sour milk.

Ted Roads

Stray Bomb

I had a super childhood, living at Lillingstone Dayrell. Rationing affected us a bit, but we had an advantage living in the country. There was the odd stray bomb, but no serious damage. We'd cycle in to see films at the Chandos, leaving our bicycles in Ganderton's cycle shop, all jammed in his shed. We all carried a cycle repair kit in case of emergency. The Chandos was an improvement on the town hall where Mrs Webb used to play piano in time to the excitement of the plot. I remember watching Dorothy Lamore, Will Hey and Bob Hope. It

Verney Junction 2 May 1936. The station was expected to be an interchange for continental traffic which never came. (I.P./H.C.)

Dandy Robinson, teenage cabaret dancer, bottom right, with London colleagues. (D.R.)

was 7d on the balcony and 4d in the stalls.

Joe Pallett

A Town! Oh Yes Please!

I'd worked as a dancer in Cabaret on the London circuit since I was very young. My mother used to change my age according to the job. In those days you had to be eighteen to do cabaret. When war came along it stopped us doing anything. We came to Buckingham because a London neighbour had friends in Padbury and said see if you can get evacuated to Buckingham because it's a town. As Londoners we thought 'A town, oh yes please!'

Off Ration

Buckingham, being in the farming community, escaped the worst of rationing. My brother came here on leave from the RAF and was invited to dinner at the Wheatsheaf. One brought a turkey off ration.

F.R. Markham

On Our Own

My first memory of war was Neville Chamberlain, broadcasting. I knew what was going on and thought, thank goodness we know where we are now! My parents didn't feel the same way, my father had been in the Boer war and hadn't liked it. The older generation knew what it was like. We received gas masks in 1938 and there were classes on how to use them and what signals ARP would give for air raid warnings. The first warning came quickly and we thought, surely they can't be starting already. It was triggered by one unidentified aircraft. Everyone was a bit nervous. We had nowhere to hide except the neighbour's cellar. The ARP used to ride around on bicycles with these rattles and you knew there was going to be a gas attack. Church bells were to be rung in the event of an invasion.

Stockings were scarce, like most luxuries. I remember going to dances using make-up on my legs. I used to get my father to draw a line with an eyebrow pencil, down the back of my leg, to look like a seam. I never thought about asking him to do it and he never complained. He could draw. My mother would say, 'Oh, I can't draw a straight line.' It was such fun getting ready for dances. We girls went on our own.

Pip Brimson (née Beck)

End Of Road

So we got out at the station and asked somebody, 'Where's the town?' We thought it might be about three doors up! We kept walking and walking. My mother said, 'Where is this town?' So I said,' I don't know, maybe it's at the end of this road.' But we still saw no evidence. So we asked. 'Oh, it's just up over the bridge.' Then we saw these people around the town hall. Miss Fleischman, the evacuee officer, was on a horse. We looked very dishevelled because we'd been down the London Underground sheltering from bombs for two nights and we had the cat in a basket. My mother was deaf and hadn't quite understood when she was told to register at the old workhouse. To say workhouse to her was an insult. She was ready to pull Miss Fleischman off her horse. I said, 'It's all right, it's the name of a building that's been taken over for registering evacuees'. 'Oh!' she said.

So Little Here!

We couldn't get over it. We were still looking for the town. There was so little here. No Woolworths! We walked on down through the town to register and we were still looking for the shops. We found out afterwards that every shop had people related to people in the next shop. If you went in one and couldn't get something, then went in another and complained about the first shop, the lady would say, 'that's my aunt!'

Dandy Robinson

Suffered

I was born in Brackley and moved to Mixbury. I was called up on the 1 September 1939. I

William G. Beck, c. 1938.

wasn't pleased, I knew it was coming and thought we'd got to go. There were quite a few of us from around Buckingham. I knew them and that was better than going off on your own. I had some of my best mates killed in Sicily but didn't go overseas myself until D-Day. I was twenty-three when I came back. A lot of people suffered.

Harry Claridge

Doctor a Doctor

Dr Ciresto came during the war. Before that we had Dr Hicks at Maids Moreton. A doctor was a doctor in those days. Surgery was open till eight o'clock at night and if you worked you couldn't get there before seven o'clock. It was a very small place and you had to pay but not much. They didn't give you pills in those days. It was all medicines. You'd go to get it and it would be laying on the table with your name on it, you didn't go to the chemist.

Certificate

Coming from a big family, my mum never had to pay for the doctor, he let her off. In those days Dr Lodge had a certificate because he had water trouble. He could get out and do it at the side of his car!

Bert Woodfield

Coming And Going

When the war started there were army camps in the area. Something to do with directing traffic and assembling convoys. They had accommodation in the old post office. The old post office became the food office. We used to see a lot of coming and going. There was a searchlight battery just up the Northampton road, near Maids Moreton.

Never Knew

We never really knew what was going on during the war.

Iris Claridge

What Work?

I signed on for the army but they asked me what work I did. I was driving eight-wheelers for the London Brick Company then. They said, 'We'll keep you out because we need heavy goods drivers.' I used to cart parts of tanks from where they were made up north and bring them down to High Wycombe. They were artful during the war. They never completed a thing in one place. Tanks were tested at High Wycombe and tyres were synthetic rubber and the weight could make them pop. I had four go. The fuel was made from coal.

Bill Tomkins

Very Romantic

Later on there were the RAF OTUs (Operational Training Units). All the airmen used to come to the dances. We

Pip Beck walks away after her farewell to this young soldier outside Barclays Bank in 1939. (P.B.)

loved that, it was fantastic, dancing with somebody with a brevet on, especially wings. They weren't just sophisticated, there was this sense that they had a wider knowledge of things. They came from somewhere different and were different. They were generally more intelligent. Air crew were picked for their intelligence. It was very romantic, we'd see a few of them again if they were stationed at Bicester. It was very romantic, but it was difficult to start a serious romance because most weren't there for any length of time.

Sad, Not Heartbroken

Occasionally you'd see a sailor in uniform, home on leave and the papers used to print casualty lists. I went out with a RAF Air Gunner, he lived in Wicken. He used to write to me and one day he didn't. I was sad, but not heartbroken. It made me aware.

Few Bombs

A few stray bombs fell in the area, accidentally or when planes were being chased. There was one at Stowe which broke all the windows down the front but not many around the town There were a few sandbags to absorb the blast. I remember falling over some. when I came on duty to the ARP centre. I joined the report and control centre as a telephonist. I said I was eighteen and didn't just want to be a messenger, even though that was an important job. Our skills weren't tested waiting by the phone for air raid warnings. Warnings were usually purple,

which meant a distant prospect of enemy aircraft. Usually they passed straight over.

The raid on Coventry was the only Red warning I recall. That night you could see the glow from high spots in Buckingham. The local fire brigade went to that but there wasn't a lot of news about it in the paper because of security. We youngsters found it all very exciting.

I remember noting in my diary that I was cross that we weren't doing enough and blamed the government for not being more prepared.

In My Head

The Battle of Britain gave me the idea to join the WAAFs. I just wanted to be doing something and wasn't old enough. I had to wait until 1941. My parents weren't keen, but my friend Joyce and I both wanted to join. She was also an only child like I was and we had the same sort of difficulty. So I said to my parents, 'we don't want to end up working in a factory, you know what armament factories are like.' So, reluctantly they agreed. One of the ARP controllers agreed to take us down to Oxford in his car. All we wanted to do was get in there. I hadn't finished my hairdresser's training, Mother was quite ill and I was needed at home. My friend Joyce was working in Smith's and could just leave.

Might Miss It!

We signed on at Oxford, where they asked us what we could do – neither of us

A few bombs fell but flooding did its usual to annoy as seen here in Nelson Street in 1941. Bert Williams brings tea to relieve suffering. Butchers apprentice, George Baderick is distinguished by his apron. (J.S)

had a great deal to offer. The recruiting officer thought about it and said, 'I know, there's a job just opened for WAAFs as RT (Radio Telephone) operators. We had no idea what it was, but we said 'Oh yes please!' We didn't leave immediately, we weren't called up until August 1941. We thought we might miss the war. Eventually we got to training station; square bashing. We went to Bridgnorth in Shropshire. We had warrants and directions by train to Birmingham, were met by WAAF NCOs to escort us to the next train, and then we were bussed to camp. We were overawed, there were so

many long huts and long black asphalt paths. We thought, 'What have we done?'

Clothes Off!

We had to go through various tests. It was quite embarrassing really because you practically had to take all your clothes off for a medical examination. None of us were used to that sort of thing but we were all in the same boat. We had various injections. Stories went around the camp that the needles were really blunt. We got there, sleeves rolled up, they plunged the needle in. It wasn't too bad. I saw one airman pass out and our arms were a bit sore. We went on to more complicated courses, and all sorts of PE. Then we were on to an operational airfield, trained by the airmen we were replacing. I never fancied being an NCO and taking parades. We weren't bullied by them but we were a bit afraid because they had authority. I never met an NCO I was particularly taken with.

Too Much

On the way back the excitement proved too much and I was sick. I was so ashamed but they were terribly nice. They said, 'Don't worry, it happens to anybody.' Poor old ground crew had to clear it up.

Persuaded

We weren't supposed to get too close to officers but you got friendships. You had to be careful not to be seen. If people were attracted they'd find ways round the rules. Air crew were not supposed to take WAAFs into aircraft but I persuaded a Canadian to take me up, smuggling me in among his crew who were quite tall. We were flying low level formation and close together. Lancasters have large wings and it looked as if we were inches apart. But they were very skillful and experienced pilots. They said I must wear a helmet in case anyone looked in and saw my curls. It was fantastic. I was only up for about an hour. Wonderful seeing cattle running away, and this tremendous roaring of the engines. We saw a farm

worker just throw himself down on the ground in absolute terror. It was great, I'd wanted to fly since the day I'd arrived on station.

Pip Brimson (née Beck)

A Lot Of Girls

I think it was John Butler said to me, 'We've got a lot of girls here, can you teach them something?' They're taught differently nowadays, but we did things like high kicking with all the girls in line. We used to start early in the morning and work for four hours. We put on various shows at the town hall. We couldn't get costumes during the war so we

Mrs Beck.

bought dusters from Vyles. They found me a lot of blue and white check and we had them make them up into skirts. Betty Pateman was one of the evacuees who was very vocal, She said, 'You're not telling me what to do. How old are you?' 'None of your business, get on and do your work,' I said. They turned out ever such nice girls.

Dandy Robinson

My Honour

I met Harry when he was in the army during the war. His mother kept the shop in her front room at Mixbury, a few miles west of Buckingham. I first went there in 1943. We had a train from Oxford and a taxi from Finmere. Everybody came to the shop to buy something so that they could see what I looked like! They killed a pig in my honour. Meat was rationed, but we had it every day at Mixbury. My sister Iris came to visit and said, 'Look at all our Iris's meat!' I'd got the hams hung over our range. That was unheard of in the towns.

Mrs I. Claridge

Steamed Up

I hitch hiked home during the war. people were good. I always got lifts. Mother worried and insisted I went back by train the first time I came home. But everyone hitched and I didn't know anyone who'd had trouble. You could walk up to people you'd never met if they were just getting into their car and just say, 'excuse me are you going to...', wherever you wanted to go. They'd say, 'Yes, hop in.' I've stood at the

roadside and never had a problem, getting lifts with all sorts. One was a Canadian in a wireless truck. I got a lift to Hinton in the Hedges from near Buckingham and he was pushing this thing along, with steam pouring from the bonnet. I said, 'Don't you think you should get some water?' He said, 'It's not mine, I don't care.' I think he just about made it.

Get In, Hon!

Another time, I was in Oxford and I thumbed some American lorries going my way. One stopped. The driver was black. He said, 'Oh, get in, hon.' So, I got in and he drove like the wind through Oxford. I was really frightened. He turned round to me

Land Army Girls at work, Thornborough Mill, c. 1943. (F.T.)

Young WAAF Pip Beck.

Young Warrior Harry Claridge takes time off for his wedding. (H.C.)

and said, 'You frightened honey?' I said, 'No!' Americans were like that. I remember another lift when I was stationed at Barfoot St Johns just outside Banbury. I was stuck in the back seat with a couple of others and there was a driver passing round bottles of cider. They offered it to me, I wasn't used to drink and didn't really want it so I just pretended. At one stage they went right up a high bank at the side of the road. I thought this won't do. So I'm going to be terribly English and put on my best WAAF officer's voice and said 'Would you mind not doing that please!' Some Americans did show off, they could be very brash but several were just the opposite. One wanted me to marry him, but I didn't want to go to America. I kept in touch with him and his mother. Mothers must have had

a dreadful time worrying about their families miles from home during the war.

Congealed Egg!

Food was adequate. Occasionally we got a congealed fried egg. Air crew got the best for their operational suppers and deserved everything they got.

Pip Brimson (née Beck)

CHAPTER 3
Back to the Past

Old Gaol, 1930s. After the war this scene was little changed. (P.B.)

Back To The Past

Originally Wilby's coal business belonged to a Mr Lamboume up the Stratford road. Then my dad ran it through the war years. Afterwards he went into partnership with his brother Ted. It was my uncle who suggested I did dancing lessons because I was always full of life and leaping about. As a little girl I went around with my dad in the lorry. Sunday mornings I'd go with him down the yard as a grease monkey. My older brother went into it after National Service.

Kind Heart

I was happy at school Mr Bodenham the headmaster was fair. Miss Bertram, the

Dandy Robinson, second from right, back row, and pianist Ron Mead with dancers. Town Hall in the late 1940s. (S.W.)

headmistress was a strong Catholic, taking a Catholic class while we had assembly. If it hadn't been for her I wouldn't have coped when my brother died. She had a kind heart.

Eastern Promise

I started my dancing with Dandy Robinson aged three and a half she did acrobatic dancing. She lived up Gawcott Road. We went to concerts all over the place, travelling on Yang Yang's bus. I came away from the London Sunshine Homes concert with an honours award. Dandy's mother wore a lot of black, she looked very Victorian, a very upright lady. She always came with us. But Dandy gave up ballet

and so I transferred to Monica Taylor's school at Brackley where I did tap and ballet. We did a performance at Winslow in the early 1950s, a musical called *The Rich Maharajah of Magador*. We were doing the Eastern Promise dance in flowing trousers and just a piece of material across our boobs. Most of the girls lost this material during the dance but we just went off stage, pinned the material back and carried on dancing. I turned professional at seventeen and gave up at nineteen to get married. I didn't think my stage career and marriage were compatible because you were on the road so much. I've worked with some well known names. I did a tour with Peter Brough and Archie Andrews. Bill Maynard was one of my favourites. He was always full of fun. I was on the phone to my boyfriend one night and Bill grabbed the phone to say, 'Don't believe her, she's having a great time!' I enjoyed my time on stage. There were never any jealousies and the girls were certainly not bimbos. We had some brilliant times but I never missed it.

Sheila Wilkes (née Wilby)

Lost!

I wanted to go back to London after the war, I'd been looked on as an oddity here with my London accent. Mother was a strict disciplinarian and was the driving force behind my stage career. When she became ill I started to teach and when she died I was in my twenties and lost without her. I went up to London to do a pantomime. I was very thin, not eating or sleeping. This lady said she couldn't take the risk and I came out utterly dejected, seeing these people crowding along the road near another theatre I thought there must be an audition. They wanted somebody to do acrobatics and ballet. I got the job. But my landlady Mrs Allen said if you don't come back to Buckingham you'll lose your cottage. So I decided not to go on dancing and went to the scent factory, labelling bottles and boxing them. The supervisor said, 'You'll have to be quicker.' I did a lot and had one bottle left. She said, 'Where did you get these labels from? This isn't jasmine!' I'd labelled them all wrong. So I decided that wasn't the life for me and went to the box factory next to Markham's, behind the White Hart; which was even worse.

Dandy Robinson

Russian Dance

This old chap – one of the travelling people, I think – used to come in the Britannia pub. I remember these two young blokes who knew him, joking about, they hid his beer money until he did this Russian dance. You wouldn't have thought he was so old if you saw him move, legs flying! Pubs were lively places in those days.

Des Tunks

Regular Soldier

I was a regular soldier. My time was up. I needed a job and somewhere to live. In those days you didn't get much help and had to look all over the country. There

Dandy Robinson getting into character. (D.R.)

was a job in accounting at the paint factory and I thought I could do it. I'd worked in a bank briefly. Accommodation was available in two stone cottages opposite Markham's. I drove up in my car, a 1934 Singer. I parked it on the corner outside Lloyd's Bank, walked across to the White Hart and said; 'Can you tell me where the town is?' 'This is it,' they said I thought, oh my God, what have I come to? The population was about 4,000. We were in the cottage about three years then moved to one of four houses built in Western Avenue especially to attract so-called management. Buckingham was very agricultural. We had the post office and W.H. Smith's manager as neighbours.

Alan Britton

Different

I remember going to the fair just after the war. There's been a charter fair here, all along the main road and round the square for over 450 years. There was this boxing booth and I was very tempted to try my luck. I'd done a bit during the war in the army and my uncle had won money at it. But I decided to leave that behind me. I had an uncle who'd been a sergeant in the Horse Artillery in India. If the Indians didn't do as they were told he'd kick 'em up the backside. When he came to Tingewick camp he tried the same method and had to leave. Things were going to be different after the war.

Des Tunks

Buckingham Railway station looking toward Banbury in March 1955 and milk churns from the neighbouring dairy await collection. (R.M.C.)

MORE POWER TO THE MINX!

NEW FULLY-PROVED PLUS-POWER ENGINE

gives you MORE *Speed* AT THE GETAWAY ..

MORE *Power* ON THE HILLS ..

The Hillman Minx ... a full size family car famous for its comfort and reliability ... gives you still better performance, yet running costs are as low as ever!

THE HILLMAN

MINX MAGNIFICENT

SALOON · CONVERTIBLE COUPÉ · ESTATE CAR
SALOON £395
plus purchase tax

A PRODUCT OF THE ROOTES GROUP

Agents—

PHILLIPS & SONS (Buckingham) Ltd

Motor Works, Buckingham

Phone—Buckingham 2121   Telegrams—Phillips Buckingham

The modern image of postwar popular motoring. (B.W.A.)

Us Old Ones

There aren't many of us old ones left to remember life before the war. Unions at Calvert made it almost a closed shop, they got our pay rises and were more or less telling the capitalists where to get off. People expected big improvements after the war, especially the blokes who'd come out of the army.

Arthur Chilton

Like My Dad

I finished school at fourteen and the normal thing would have been for me to go to work on the Robart's estate like my dad, working in the garden. The chauffeur, Mr Gosling, said to dad, 'What's Joe going to do? How about I have a word with Phillips?' It was either that or RAF Halton as an apprentice. I got 7s 6d a week as an apprentice. When I got married at twenty two I was earning £6 10s a week.

Proud

We were so proud when we did a complete engine overhaul. It would probably take a week. You don't hear of grinding valves or anything like that now. The bill would be about £17 10s. A reconditioned engine would cost about £24 in 1951/52. Engines were much simpler. They've advanced a lot over the last twenty years with ignition systems and better materials.

Joe Pallett

Vicar Came

The vicar came along and said, 'Miss Robinson, what are you doing here in the box factory, you're better off working with your feet.' But I went to another factory in Tingewick Road where they made parts for buses. It was a terrible job drilling and lacquering this metal, it made me terribly sick. I wasn't eating, I used to walk round town all night long, still grieving for my mother. I thought I'd have to do something so I joined the civil service in Tingewick road. I missed my dancing though. I had one or two pupils. I went back to teaching voluntarily in the end.

Dandy Robinson

Good Left Back

Charlie Twelvetrees was dedicated to the football club. It was his life. He had all the information in his head and was the nicest chap you could hope to meet. He was on the Berks and Bucks FA and used to play football for Buckingham. He was a good left back.

Des Tunks

Wide Spectrum

I was a prisoner of the Japanese during the war. In December 1951 I came to work in my uncle, Charles Evenson's business. Having been a buyer for a builder's merchant, I knew the form. I'd spent many holidays in the town. I married the

Buckingham Town football, early post war years at Ford Meadow. (N.T.)

following year and we settled down in a flat in Prebend House. We had a wide spectrum of customers, being in the town and serving farmers before Cooper's or Brown's. There were gentlemen farmers and tenant farmers. They all had credit accounts and sometimes it was difficult to get the cash out of people after three months. I knew all the characters in town. One of my staff, Bernie Clarke worked well into his eighties. He'd been a farmhand on a small holding. Mr Evenson ran the business until he died in 1961. The first man I saw on television was Aiden Crawley, Labour MP just after the war. One of our relations, Fred Markham from Aylesbury, invited us over to watch Mr Crawley speaking.

Screens were big if they were twelve inches in those days. Of course, Mr Crawley moved with the times and packed up politics to go into television work.

Austerity

That was a time of austerity. Buckingham was lucky being close to the farming community, being protected from the worst of rationing. My wife came from a mining area of South Wales where it was harder.

F.R. Markham

West Street, 1960, and very few cars on show. The road is now a busy cut through. (I.B.)

Funny Customers

I got fed up with drawing the bricks at Calvert and asked the manager for a job driving the new fork lift hoister trucks to get the bricks out of the kilns. Just after I'd given in my notice he offered me the yard foreman's job but it was too late, I'd signed up to run Twyford village shop. I didn't know the first thing about the business when I started in 1955. It was run down.

I had some funny old customers. One chappie said, 'Old Percy's puttin' oranges in his pocket.' I watched and he'd got a hole in his pocket and they fell out and rolled along the floor. so he had to pick 'em up. I said to my assistant, 'When he comes in again, keep an eye on him.'

Old Percy

When he came in he put a packet of biscuits in his pocket. Then he went out. Outside the shop was a sill and he was sat on it. I sat next to him and said, 'Percy, you got a packet of biscuits in your pocket you didn't pay for.' Cor, he was a queer old boy. He stood up, saying 'You accusing me of having biscuits?' I said, 'Yes'. He said, 'I'm going to get my solicitor on you!' I said, 'Fair enough, Percy.' There was a phone kiosk over by The Crown. I said to my assistant, 'Give me a copper or two, I'm off to the phone. I'm going to ring up my solicitor.' Old Percy got up off that sill, he went off down that road like a March Hare. He never came in again for a long time.

Stan Beckett

54

Their Bodies Were All Right!

One day someone said to me, 'Have you ever had pheasant?' I said, 'Oh Yes.' With my husband working on the railway, we had them because the birds used to have their dust baths and trains used to knock their heads off, but their bodies were all right as long as the men got to them before the crows. You generally got them at dusk or first thing. They were beautiful. Harry used the feathers to clean his pipe.

Iris Claridge

Simple Things

Alf Beckett was a plate layer at Verney Junction. He came into the cabin one morning and said about all the chicken he'd had the night before and the left overs were in his sandwiches for his lunch. He'd say he hadn't time to shave so I said, 'Do the same as I do, wipe the oven stick on and wipe it off in the morning.' He was a fatish simple, red-in-the-face sort of bloke and laughed like the devil at simple things, we were always pulling each others legs. Working on the railway line there was a lot of old wood the railway didn't want but if we did we had to pay for it, whether it was old fencing, sleepers or branches. We had a trolley, called the bogie, to carry things around along the line. We pushed it. I'd borrow that on a Sunday, when there were no trains, to carry wood home to Station Terrace or fetch my potatoes from the allotments. I even brought my aviary home from Westfield on it.

Des Tunks

Fulwell and Westbury Station Crossing, March 1955. (R.M.C.)

Verney Junction, March 1955. (I.P./R.M.C).

Time Warp

Buckingham was a little place in a time warp, as though nothing had happened. They dressed old fashioned. There were people like Walter Tyrell who had the local way of speaking and travelled with a donkey and cart. He'd tell you he'd never been to the seaside. He was about seventy. How can a man get to that age and not see the sea? To me that was Buckingham. That's what attracted people to it. Locals used to call it the lost marshes of North Oxford! When we used to travel back from my wife's home town, and over, at weekends, once north of Oxford there was no traffic. You could go through Bicester and not see a light and you had to make sure you had enough petrol after Oxford!

Little Notes

The paint factory at the junction of Tingewick Road and Nelson Street was all Nissen Huts. Tom Mallett and I used to go to auctions for a lot of the stuff. If you were starting up a business in those days you had trouble getting furniture. We went to Ministry of Supply sales where they sold surplus furniture. We bought our first cars and lorries at Doddington. Bill Howkins came with me. You'd put a note on a vehicle bonnet saying 'Cracked block' to put the bidders off. Come the auction we were the only ones who wanted it! If you wanted a bit of furniture, you put a little note 'Woodworm' so no one else was interested. The Nissen huts came from near Gosport. We used to bid by the door numbers We switched door numbers to get the best hut. We got the despatch department that way. We had to, after the war, businesses were working on a shoe string. Our premises were at Castle Mill on Fisher's Field, a stream ran through the middle of the works. Bill Howkins literally built that. He'd been in the Royal engineers during the war. He built that to last. I think he got the girders from a bombed out cinema in Birmingham. in those days nearly everybody was ex-service of some sort and you applied your particular skills. A little road train pulled by a Lister used to pull trailers loaded with paint from the mill to despatch. Big Hedley Carter drove it at one time. His wife had a shop at Maids Moreton. A number of people came and went in those early days. One chemist, Alex Mackintosh lasted only a year or two. Michael Richardson – the firm was E. & F. Richardson – hired a variety of people who appeared and disappeared. I thought of him as a sort of run down Maxwell type. He stood for the general election in the 1950s as a conservative candidate. I went with him to help. Michael was more interested in things outside the factory. I spent three to four years visiting with him on his yacht down in Cornwall. We hardly did a full week's work in those days. Time on the yacht, it was all part and parcel of why I liked the place. Michael was in his early forties, fairly fit – he played table tennis. He got me to join the volunteer fire brigade with him, we used to have these bells to call us out at home, otherwise we'd down tools at work and rush off when we heard the siren. His father lived up at Maids Moreton Manor, that was his garden. Michael lived at Radclive and ran the farm from there. I was always getting phone calls when it was hay-making season, to take people away from the factory to help out. When it was fruit picking, old man Richardson would phone up, 'I want two men to help pick blackcurrants,' and when they had finished he'd make them poke their tongues out! He'd knock sixpence off their wages if he found their tongues stained!

Alan Britton

Out Of The Army

When I came out of the army I was going back to my old job working in the gardens, with a tied cottage, under Mr Morton, an old boy at Tingewick Hall. A friend of mine said, 'Keep away from it, life has gone for the gardeners.' So I decided to go on to the railway. I had to go up to Winslow to the Permanent Way Inspector's Office for an interview. I was put on the Fulwell and Westbury gang, working from about a quarter mile on the Buckingham side of Brackley to Verney Junction. There were six or seven of us and the ganger was Jack Rollins who lived in a cottage at Radclive. Des Tunks joined the gang twelve months after me because he came out of the army later. The first time I met my ganger, Jack Rollins, on the railway, he said, 'Can you set a snare?' I said, 'No'. He said, 'That's the first job you've got to learn and you've got the best bloke in the country, Fred Aries, to teach you.' Fred used to set snares all along the lengths of our line and sell them to the drivers. We'd come in early to snare.

Vermin

Phil Rush set a snare just up the line from Fulwell and Westbury, in the hedge, and

Monica Taylor's Dancing, Town Hall, 1948. Grace Durham (née Walton) is front centre. (G.D.)

caught a pheasant. That was marvellous. We done a good job keeping the vermin down.

Fiddling

I was a porter at Fulwell and Westbury, they were hilarious days. I used to grow and sell Christmas trees there as a sideline. I'm still owed for three from 1950! I used to do a bit of fiddling. If someone wanted something, I'd get vegetables and all sorts. This old boy came through on the eleven o'clock night train. He said, 'Are you on?' The guard went for tea with Arthur Marriot in the signal box while we were busy and then the train left without him and had to reverse all the way back! Fred Kimble was in charge of the station. I don't think he liked me They were steam days, drivers used to throw us lumps of coal. I was riding home with coal on my autocycle one night. Then I saw this blue flashing light, I thought Christ they've got me. Turned out my wife had called them because I was late and she was worried. We needed our perks because the pay wasn't good.

Religion

Fred Kimble was a religious man so he wouldn't approve of any unauthorised practices! But there was all sorts going on. The signal box was the place to place your bets. They had a bookie's runner. Railwaymen were a religion on their own. People helped each other.

Des Tunks

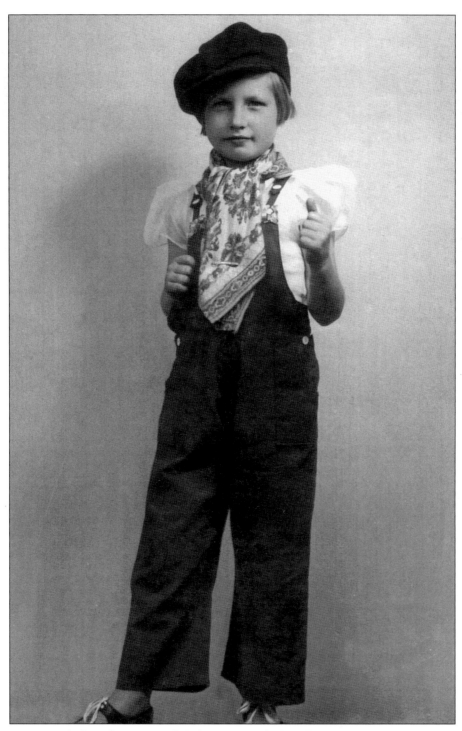

Sheila Wilkes (née Wilby) doing the Lambeth Walk, c. 1946. (S.W.)

Buckingham Station facing Verney Junction, March 1955. Mr Marsh the bookie's runner is on the platform far right. Behind him appears to be newsreader Richard Baker on a poster advertising Brylcream.

Potato Wine

My wife used to make wine from potatoes, parsnips and dandelions. My dahlia's went all over the country. An old boy used to come inspecting from Derby. 'I'd love some,' he said. 'How much are they?' Had a plot to the side of the station, planted and sold them to everybody. It was a different way of life.

Solid Truth

Christmas 1947 there was a hard frost which lasted 'til March and they forecast snow. A mail train used to reach Fulwell and Westbury about 5.15 p.m. If the weather was bad they'd get us out the night before to clear the snow. Fred Aries and me booked on at five this particular morning because of the snow forecast. We got the train through and thought it wasn't worth going back home. In the afternoon it started snowing again so they sent a light engine down from Bletchley to keep running up and down to keep it clear. Then we heard it was stuck near Farthingoe. They said they'd bring a ballast train and told us not to go home because we'd got to go on it. Well it got stuck. The blizzard blew right under the train and set as hard as iron. We carried on digging out the light engine. We had this ever such a little chap Billy Bull, and it's the solid truth, he walked into this snow and all you could see was his hat! Those engine drivers could see that no matter what, they weren't going to get home. When we got through to Brackley the canteen was shut, so we weren't going to get anything to eat. We got back to Fulwell and Westbury at five or six the next morning, up to our waist in snow.

Harry Claridge

Sledge

We had to shovel the snow away before we could shut the door. The butcher brought the meat from Brackley on a sledge.

Iris Claridge

Stormy Weather

Tom Aries and I walked to Buckingham the next day. Those cuttings were a picture.

later that week there was a terrible gale and rain. It blew some chimneys off and there was flooding. My dad was a sort of foreman/roadman, digging a way out. We were among the few people who worked then, it was so bad.

Red Carpet

I had to walk the length of our line when the King and Queen came down in 1951, and stand at this mile post to signal to him that the length was clear. Men came to help break off all the branches. They had gangers and inspectors out looking under every bridge, examining everything. Tom Aries, the ganger at Brackley, had to stand on the platform at Westbury and the engine driver had to stop dead opposite him so that the King, Queen and Princess got out of the

Fulwell and Westbury Station, facing Banbury, 12 December 1955. (R.M.C.)

61

compartment exactly in line with the red carpet. But they hadn't estimated that the platform was lower than expected and needed an ammunition box for them to climb down on to. They went back by car.

Perfect

All the stations were kept perfect. The people at Westbury Manor provided plants for Westbury station. People liked to see it. The station gardeners were very particular. They did it because they liked to see it.

Harry Claridge

Unsophisticated

The paint factory was started by E. & F. Richardson. Michael's first name was Francis. They came here from Mitcham in Surrey when war was imminent. Paint manufacture could be done on a gravity basis. You had varnish at the top and pigments in the middle. It wasn't very sophisticated. That's why old mills like ours were popular. They bought Castle Mill, Nelson Street in 1938.

Camouflage

During the war, Richardson's got the contract for camouflage paints. Because of that he didn't have to go into the services, which may have bothered him. I remember him knocking on the back door. He'd picked up a hitch hiker from somewhere and asked if I would I take him back to his barracks. On the way the airman was saying, 'He's a

fantastic chap, your boss, fighter pilot and all that.' That was Michael. He could have been a good actor. He was a bit of a Maxwell, always seemed to get his picture in the paper when he went abroad. Ambition perhaps.

Alan Britton

Fun

I bought the Bell Garage in 1952 which at one time had been run by the Bell Hotel in Winslow. I bought it off Peter Curtiss who carried on working for me. I remember we had an old Hillman Minx down the side of the garage and Peter said we ought to start it up so that we could sell it. We got a battery and turned it over. No good so we poured some petrol down the air cleaner. All of a sudden it backfired, caught the can of petrol alight that was in Peter's hand. He threw it in the road right in front of a man coming along on his bike. Lucky it didn't hit him, but we did get it started! We were right on the main road which was often busy. Mr Wigley senior used to have to drive across to get petrol. We'd stand there directing him. He was very, very deaf and would sit in the road in this old Austin 10. By the time he'd got it in gear there was something else coming, so we'd say, 'Stop!' and he'd say 'You said go'. He'd ring up a night or two later and say, 'Mr Brazier, would you come over, the car's in the rose bushes.' He'd had one too many. We'd go over to Steeple Claydon and get it out. We had some fun in those days. Cars were still pretty basic. There was no unleaded petrol. You were mostly taking the heads off, de-carbonising and putting new valves in. The old Austin

7s didn't do more than 40 mph – the same as most cars.

Les Brazier

Best Thing

I came to Tingewick Army camp in 1955, on detachment from Bulford near Salisbury. The best thing about that was I met my wife. I was an ambulance driver. It wasn't as busy as Bulford where we used to meet some terrible cases. There were some real psychiatric cases. There was one WRASC woman who had to be held down in the ambulance because she was going potty. The services always had that problem. They used to shoot them in the First World War. We've a lot to be thankful for today! At Tingewick we slept in the back of the ambulance on a stretcher because it was comfortable and the RSM couldn't get in to wake us up in the morning. He used to bang away on the door! My mate was courting a girl in Preston Bissett and I came down the village with him. Sometimes we came in the ambulance, sometimes on his girl's bike. He pedalled and I sat on the saddle. One foggy night we went through the bridge. I fell for the girl next door, my mate's girlfriend. Coming to Tingewick was the best thing that ever happened to me.

Bob Tyzack

When I Was Young

I started at Well Street School when I was five. I remember I took the old dog with me. He got stuck under the desk and didn't want

The road south into Buckingham, 1947. (A.G.)

Bert Williams, Joy Sterner's dad, c. 1928. They won the special prize most years. (J.S.)

to get out. Me mate Vincent tickled off. He said, 'I ain't stoppin' here.' Then I went to the senior school which was all right if you liked football. I didn't. When me dad died there were five of us still at school. He was forty-nine, worked all hours, had his own haulage business. Mum carried on and me brother Keith took it over in 1965. We'd all took our turns when me brother was on holiday. We had the pigs up our field. Hauled anything, cattle, coal from the goods yard to the army camp, parcels as well. Everyone did parcels. We took coal to Thornton College and Stowe. I had a motorbike when I was young. I used to ride it 'round the field. My first bike was a Royal Enfield 125, then a Francis Barrett 175 and then a 500 AJS and then a 600 AJS. I sold the last one for £50 when it was worth £1800 new.

Derek Knibbs

Varney's Little Coach

Varney had some funny old buses. There was one we called the old salmon tin. He hit the lamp post outside Doris Martin's café. The firm petered out in the end, people wouldn't book him.

Des Tunks

Dressed Up

There was old man Varney and his son Alf. Mother and father loved going on their coach trips after the war. This particular Thursday they were going to Ascot. They went down to pick the bus up in the market square. When they got on the bus Alf was there dressed up to take them out. Old man Varney used to come along and see them off and this day he looked at Alf and said, 'You can take that suit off, you got my suit on.' And the old man made him go back and change. Alf was a character. If he'd been out to the seaside he'd pull up in some lay by and say, 'Toilets, gentlemen on the right, ladies on the left!'

Bert Woodfield

Rough Lot

I worked in the King's Head in the late 1950s. There was a rough lot got in there. I used to help out at the Swan and Castle too. The old parson from Whittlebury was a regular there. One night some old boy was making a do and the police were expected. This old Irish man went over the bar like a stag Rocky Hollis came through to the tap bar and said, 'Have you seen Revd Fred in here?' I went through and this old fat boy was in there with a dirty shirt and fag (cigarette). I said, 'Do you know if the Revd Smith is in here?' He said, 'I am the Revd Smith.' He was pie-eyed so we took him home.

Phillip 'Pedro' Rush

Rivalry

Alf Varney always spat. They called him 'Spitter'. He'd spit at me if he met me. We had a bit of rivalry between his and my bus on Buckingham Fair night because we picked up a lot of his passengers coming through Newton Purcell.

Bert Woodfield

Yang Yang

We called Alf Varney 'Yang Yang'. He wore an old mac and a cap. They called that road up to his garage 'Yang Yang's' toilet.

Des Tunks

How It Was

My first memory of the cinema was Sunday night at the Chandos. We saw one of those American musicals. We hadn't our own TV and I'd only seen the tiny screen of a neighbour's; I was amazed by this huge colour picture and all the sound. When it finished my mother held me back to stand and listen to some music while an image of a red coated lady rode a horse across the screen with some soldiers. It turned out to be the national anthem and the queen. Of course, that all seems silly in today's flashy multi cultural society, but that's how it was.

Robert Cook

Broken Nose

My grandfather made me a pedal car, it had a proper opening door and a cut down Austin 7 engine block. When my brother Michael was old enough he had to make do with a bought second-hand one and he didn't like that. He pushed me out of mine one day and broke my nose. I ended up in hospital!

John Ganderton

Les Brazier, proprietor Bell Garage, Winslow, Buckingham, 1963. (L.B.)

Phillip 'Pedro' Rush (left) and Des Tunks re-united nearly forty years after working on the railway, enjoying memories, December 2000.

Grown Up

Buses were always packed on the weekends of Buckingham Fair. As a child it was an exciting place to go. The grown ups always seemed to act very silly, shouting and squealing. Of course I didn't realize they weren't that grown up, they were just teenagers all dressed up and acting big. They were in a different world to me. I just liked the opportunity to pretend to fly planes, or rockets or drive cars, buses and lorries on the roundabouts. It made me feel grown up too, but obviously in a different way!

Robert Cook

Finding Fault

I left school in 1956 and worked at the paint factory. I got £2 2s a week and gave me mother half. Mercx the boss and myself had our uppers and downers and there were others there who were always finding fault, so I went to work for Jenny Gardiner at Grove Hill Farm where the old army camp was. The army left there when I was about eighteen. I was driving a combine at sixteen and my pay was £5 4s a week. I went on to Unigate Dairies until it shut in 1965. Bert Williams left the railway to work there. Bill Betts used to go over the railway office to put his bets on. I went there as a driver going round the farms collecting milk churns. I did the Oxford area, collected off the milk stands. Then farmers had two or three churns. Robarts' with eleven was a big farm. Half the farms don't milk now. I used to go from Buckingham in the morning, up Maids Moreton Road, along to Akeley Wood School, to Deley's Farm Ratcliffe, Water Stratford, Tingewick, along Brackley Road to Turweston railway bridge. I'd have one

Alf Varney's Guy Vixen coach, just the ticket for a day trip to the races! (A.S.)

John and Michael Ganderton in John's pedal car. The family garage was then on the opposite side of the road, the cycle works and shop were behind the white frontage. (J.G.)

Advertisement in the Buckingham & Winslow Advertiser.

Buckingham Show Trade stand, c. 1957. (M.S.)

hundred and two churns on a full load. Old Ben Nicholls did Thornborough. It was a laugh a minute.

Derek Knibbs

Funny One

Old Freddie Walduck was a funny one when he retired. He'd got a chicken house along the railway line. Many's the time I'd found him asleep in there with a bottle of home made wine. One day I had him, I filled it half with water while he was asleep.

Little Austin

When I first started working for Mr Marriot at Buckingham it was 1958/59 and I got a lift in a little Austin A30. We got a bit of snow in those days and just past Hillesden there was a field gate in the hedge. The wind roared through and took us into this skid. The driver didn't know which way to turn. We went from one side of the road to the other and finished up in a ditch. We had to walk to Gawcott to say we couldn't get in and Marriots brought the old Morris Commercial to pull us out. Being out at Twyford was out on a limb in those days. We had a bus to Buckingham on Tuesdays - 'Yang Yang' Varney's utility bus. I was interested in noisy old racing cars at Silverstone but dad wasn't. It wasn't until I started working and driving in 1957 that I could get about. Then I became interested in television. It wasn't thought about much then. I modified a television to 625 lines and the first signals I got were from Czechoslovakia, then Moscow, Italy and Spain. There's a certain time of the year when there's a lot of sun spot activity and the ionosphere virtually becomes like

a metal plate collecting signals over the earth, these conditions last from May to September.

Down Your Way

Franklin Engleman brought his *Down Your Way* radio show to Buckingham in 1959. He visited our workshop at Marriot's and said there was to be no advertising. He started asking me questions and I said, 'It's a Phillips television set I use for my long distance signals.' I realized I shouldn't have said it but he said, 'Don't worry, it'll be edited out for Sunday night.' And it was, so well you didn't notice. That's the power of radio and television!

Ian Beckett

CHAPTER 4

Backing Britain

Market Square, early 1960s, and the dawn of a new era. The bus was first of three seventy-one seaters as Red Rover expanded to cope with the still high demand on the Aylesbury to Buckingham route. The sixites were soon singing and swinging, but by 1968 the trade situation was so bad there was a desperate ditty, 'I'm backing Britain' aimed to persuade us to buy British and work harder. (A.S.)

Dragon

I went to work at Brookfield Boarding house at the Royal Latin School, laying tables and then as a weekend cook. One matron was a bit of a dragon. She'd never admit to being wrong. She didn't like it when a couple of student teachers were accommodated in Brookfield and because they were told to use

her bathroom. She did go on about it. When they left, to get their revenge, they loosened the lock on her loo door so that it came off while she was in it and couldn't get out. The boys liked to shock her. They'd come out of the bathroom and do anything to torment her. There was another who was blonde, young and vivacious. She was very popular. George Embleton, the headmaster, was

West Street in July 1960. A fine array of motors when motorists were still something special. The barrel pub is on the left. (I.B.)

eccentric. I remember him going on about the fox's tail spinning round and didn't know what he was on about until I looked up and saw the weather vane.

Sheila Wilkes (née Wilby)

Planners

Buckingham was convenient for planners faced with housing needs, it attracted estate after estate, until a veritable 'doughnut' of reasonably priced housing surrounded it; and the process continues apace.

Philistine Sixties

It [Buckingham] nonetheless retained its key buildings, (in a deplorable state), and its inconvenient traffic system, losing only a little of its inconvenient traffic system in the philistine sixties. It was lucky in two respects. Having no discernible tradition for recalcitrance against authority, and no commercial base, it reacted positively to the arrival of seventies incomers who built on the core community. This strengthened and forced through major structural change – a flowering of charity, a relief road scheme, industrial development and the salvaging of its landmark buildings.

Clive Birch MBE

Honda And Hound

Paul and Steve Wheeler worked with Richard Smith on the Chackmore Chase,

Clive Birch MBE. The Observer called this former journalist, and local publisher 'man of towns' because of all the books he had written and published about towns. (J C.)

otherwise known as 'Honda and Hound'. It died not long after poor Richard did but, while it lasted, it was one of the finest examples of how to do good by doing well that ever I have seen. May it long be remembered. In sum, what they created was a meet without hounds (though Stowe beagles always turned out for show), with riders in correct costume mounted on LGPVs, who then rode the specially prepared obstacle circuit, with hilarious results. The teams were sponsored, the individuals too, and they were fined by 'Ivor the Fiver' for any infelicity of dress, real or imagined that Smithy spotted, and programmes were sold with ads, plus the Beagle Ball in the summer, to thank everyone, and raise more cash. It was all for mentally handicapped kids and it raised tens of thousands, year on year. Everyone had a great day and it did a great deal of good.

Poor Shot

There was the day I was 'Smithied'. I had a lovely dog, a black Labrador bitch called Wilkins, who was a superb peg dog, except for one thing. She was so keen, she collected everyone else's birds, and laid them all at my feel. Since I am an average poor shot, this raised suspicions and occasional temperatures. Eventually I was placed between dogless guns, so that it didn't matter, but one day Smithy decided to make a point. I got to my peg to find a golden chain attached, and a label marked 'Wilkins'. I took the hint, and secured the dog. Came the next drive, and we – made our leisurely way there, only for me to find yet another golden chain marked 'Wilkins'. This was repeated on every drive and it was only towards the end of the day that I descried a crouching Smithy stealthily soft footing it between the pegs, clutching the chain. He had been detaching and attaching the same chain all day.

Old Man Claridge

I will always remember old man Claridge. I advertised for some shooting when I first arrived, and one Saturday came a knock at the door of the hall. I was at breakfast. In he came for coffee – I had never met him before. 'You want some shooting?' 'That's right.' 'I own some land at Gawcott. You're welcome to shoot there.' After a bit, 'What would you want for that? Because shooting's really expensive.' 'Nothing really.' 'How kind.' He got up to go, 'Just one thing – you can have it if you join the Conservatives.' So it cost me a sub, I did something I had never done, as a cynical ex-journalist – I joined a political party, and I got my shooting. Or rather I didn't. In an entire season I only saw one pigeon, and that was already dead. But for years I hadn't the heart to let him down so I paid my sub, walked his fields and remained a reluctant member of a political party.

Clive Birch MBE

Lewis Cracknell holding up the Berks and Bucks Junior Football Cup in 1949. The last time that they had won the cup was in 1903.

Diesel railcars were brought in during the 1950s to make the local railway line pay, but they weren't given much chance by the road building transport minister Marples who appointed his friend Dr Beeching to close down lines and stations. (D.T)

Closures

We saw it coming in the in the 1950s. The Inspector wanted me to be ganger at Marsh Gibbon. I said, 'No'. I thought I'd get on the Great Central, but the Inspector said he wouldn't let me go. George Gibbs used to collect union subs down our way. He said, 'Leave it to me,' and a fortnight later I had a note to report to Finmere station.

Harry Claridge

Red Carpet

The Queen came on the Royal Train in the mid 1960s. We had about 35 flag men all along the bridges and gateways. The police were around Padbury for weeks and we had to clean up the bushes and path along the railway track so that she could walk the Corgis while the train was parked over night. It stopped on the Verney Junction side of Padbury. I was at Buckingham signal box and had to switch the points to bring it down along the up line, so that she could step out onto the red carpet and walk out onto Chandos Road.

Des Tunks

Sunday Opening

Father never agreed with Sunday opening but we had various charity shows. Eddy Baron ran the Baron's Grill, he'd been in the entertainment business and knew Thora Hird who lived at Hillesden. He roped her and her daughter Janette Scott, they practised at the New Inn. I think it was called *Ramsbottom and Me*. It was a very good show. But you'd never sit quiet in our cinema, there was always a disturbing element.

Gwen Harris (née Parker)

Old General

Films at the Chandos finished 10 minutes after the last bus. I remember avoiding this problem by cycling. One night I caught up with the Red Rover double-decker on the double bend just before Winslow. Old General was the driver and him and the conductor used to have a drink in the pub on Buckingham market square. Well this night General swung a bit sharp on the corner and the conductor fell off the platform at the back.

Bob Dickins

Agent

When there used to be a regular bus service to Oxford, Banbury and Northampton, my uncle started a bus parcel service. Anyone with an urgent parcel for anywhere along those routes used it. We had an official United Counties or Midland Red stamp and the conductor would collect it. That's how I was introduced to National Travel. They wanted an agent to sell tickets and they asked the United Counties controller. He said Markham looks after our

Sadly the railways were on the way out. This is Padbury on 18 March 1955, still looking pretty but not for long. (R.M.C.)

F.R Markham at work in his office, late 1970s. The National Express coach model behind him was a symbol of his busy caching agency. (F.R.M.)

parcels, he can probably organize your tickets.

F.R. Markham

Ironmonger's Institution

When I came to Buckingham, Frank Markham was an institution, running his ironmonger's. There were treasures there with pre-decimal prices, and all the age old ways of doing things: a brass counter measure; proper scales with weights and an over-riding certainty that there was always some way of giving you the service you sought.

Clive Birch MBE

Competition

The village shop at Twyford did very well over the first ten years but then, in the 1960s we began to feel the competition from supermarkets.

Stan Beckett

Princess Came

Princess Marguerite of Sweden, came to live with her husband John Ambler at Winslow Hall. She came over one day and asked if we'd look after her car. I said, certainly. She was a very nice person and had a big Volvo. It was quite a car for its day. If she wanted to go out at 9 p.m. she could set the clock at 8.45 p.m. so that when she got into it would have started up and was warm.

Les Brazier

Like Glass

The roads were like glass in the winter of 1963, but being a young lad I enjoyed sliding about, but at Steeple I got into a proper skid. The old van went gently across the road, no way was I going to stop it. I walked back to the house and phoned Marriot's. They hadn't got a tow vehicle so they called Phillip's. There wasn't a scratch on my vehicle, it had been so gentle.

Ian Beckett

Scream

We were at Buckingham fair when I heard a terrible scream. It came from the ferris wheel which was by the old gaol. I looked up and this girl had got her hair, she had a beautiful head of hair, caught up in the seat as it swirled round. They had to stop the wheel and climb up. They couldn't untangle it so they had to cut it. I asked her about it years later when she came to work at

The Black Watch Band play for the Queen Mother's visit, when she came to the Royal Latin School on 10 June 1963. Jennifer Beckett recalls them marching up Market Hill and the stirring music. They went on to play in Cornwall's meadow. (I.B.)

Stan Beckett, Autumn 1999, adjusts the radio that has served him well since the 1930s.

Hartridge's, with me. She said it felt like her head was being pulled off and how upset that they had cut her lovely hair.

Des Tunks.

Swinging

The Swinging Sixties came to us off the television, all those dangerous pop stars. You went to the Chandos cinema to see Elvis in films like *G.I. Blues*. There was Cliff Richard in *Summer Holiday* too, but he didn't quite come off in the sexy stakes. And there were no concert halls in Buckingham. So the nearest thing to dangerous entertainers were the swarthy looking fairground boys. They swaggered and looked at you in a certain way. They made you feel it was worth all the puffed out short skirts and high heels, the beehive hairdos. They didn't care if you were only fourteen, though your mother might. You didn't want to be like your mother anyway. Fairground boys made you feel like the woman you were supposed to be, especially to all that music and in the October darkness with all those flashing lights. We did some silly things. Older blokes were exciting and we wanted them to notice us. When they came with the fair, they seemed to come from far away. They were exciting.

Helen

On Fire

We stood in Hunter Street when the paint factory was on fire. The chap who did it had been sacked by Vic Watts. We joked after that that if you sacked somebody you handed them a box of matches. Mr Airey, the MD came to the fire. We stood in Hunter Street. There was a chap filming it. That was in November 1964.

Alan Britton

Blistered

I was born in Nelson Street. We'd just gone to bed and heard a bang. We thought it was a motorbike and looked out. We looked out and saw the paint factory was alight. I went across the road and got my mum out. The police turned everyone out. We stood back by the old churchyard. Them cottages down Norton Place, you couldn't put your hands on them. Our house nearly collapsed, the paint was blistered and cracked.

Derek Knibbs

All Lit Up

We were in bed, it was about eleven and we heard all this noise. When we looked out Buckingham was all lit up.

Des Tunks

Old Days

Nowadays the MP, John Bercow comes here once a month, not like the old days. Maxwell had rallies. He was a show man in the old style, a one off – just as well perhaps.

F.R. Markham

A range of the latest radios and TVs, Buckingham show, c. 1958. (M.S).

Nelson Street viewed from A.C. Marriot's Workshop – now the International Business Centre – in 1960. Today's view is much the same except for the cars. (I.B.)

Funny Little Shop

I remember it burnt the paint of my uncle's shop in Nelson Street. that was a funny little shop, called Charles Cripps (ribbons) and was run by his brother-in-law Barney, a sort of London spiv. He sold all sorts of nick-nacks including a picture device called 'Suzi's Bath night'. You could undress her by pulling this card out to make the picture change. I remember he had a big advert at the Chandos Cinema. You could buy a voice over onto a standard film. His film showed all these wonderful department store goods with this posh voice saying Charles Cripps for all your gift needs. The shop was in fact a converted front room next to Crooks' grocers. Barney used a milk bottle for a toilet. They were innocent days. But my favourite shop in Buckingham was Fishy Herring's where I got balsa wood for my model aeroplane making.

Exotic Delight

Buckingham open air swimming pool was an exotic delight to me in the 1960s as a school boy. One of the teachers who accompanied us on swimming lessons was a former air hostess who also tried in vain to teach us French. I believe her name was Mrs Teasedale; a glamorous lady who arrived for work in a Bentley. She made a glorious picture seated at the pool side chatting to an elderly maths teacher. This was so much the case that a classmate called Chris, who somehow managed to swim around wearing strong spectacles, beckoned me across the pool one afternoon to enjoy a view of her elegant legs and glimpse of stocking tops. I'm sure she must have noticed us peering up from under the overlapping paved edging. However, apparently oblivious, she gazed with tilted head, into the fine blue and sunny sky over Buckingham.

Robert Cook

Missed

When the station closed I went as a forty-one-year-old trainee to Hartridge's. From starting out as more or less a shed behind a wall, they'd won a Queen's Award to Industry for their engineering work. From a trainee making little pieces, I went on to the big machines which was more satisfying and I was training apprentices. The 550 machine went abroad to under-developed countries. Of course I missed the railway and being outdoors.

Des Tunks

Television in the Bedroom

I enjoyed my work in the radio and television business. You can't always please everybody. I've been in some homes where it's been very difficult. I went to a lady in the flats in Buckingham and the woman had drawn the curtains. Another woman in Gawcott came to the door in a see-through nightie and said, 'The television is in the bedroom'. It

Open Air Swimming pool, having become just another pile of rubble, late 1990s.

The upstairs radio and TV repair wokshop with mixed test instruments in 1960. (I.B.)

didn't worry me but some might have been dragged into a load of trouble.

Ian Beckett

Proud

I was still knitting my daughter's cardigan for the Latin school the night before she started. The shop was late getting the wool. I think Meadows' supplied all the uniform. I was very proud when she got a prize in her first year.

Gladys Cook

They Weren't Sexist

Teachers weren't sexist against the girls at the Latin School when I was there in the 1960s. They were really nice. Reggie Howard was brilliant.

Pat Chisholme (née Cook)

Don't Stint Yourself Lad!

I came for interview at the Royal Latin School in 1968, straight from university and was timid and shy. The interview was with George Embleton and there were nine other candidates, all women. I was called in first and struck a chord with George straight away. He'd played cricket for Cheshire and I'm a fanatic on County Cricket, so we started talking county cricket. Four hours later he said, 'It's time we had some lunch. Can I recommend the White Hart? We'll carry on this conversation afterwards. Don't stint yourself lad, don't stint yourself. The school will pay. Have a bottle of wine.' So I came back about half past one. 'Good to see you! Where were we? Yes,' he said, 'Cheshire 1940.' We went on for another two hours. then he said, 'Oh my God! We've got to do something about these women. I'd better talk to them. Go round the school for half an hour and come back. The job's yours of course it is, they can't play cricket but I must talk to them.'

Embarrassing

The embarrassing thing was that the nearest trains were over in Bletchley because the station had closed a few years earlier and I was taken back to the station by Edna Embleton and there were four of these ladies in the car with me. It was a somewhat difficult atmosphere. I'd got the job and they hadn't. Of course George didn't know whether I could teach maths or chemistry. I started the following September and because we'd talked so much about cricket he'd put me down to help with games. When I got to the first games lesson, I met a chap called Graham Collis, head of games and a stiff sergeant-major type. He said, 'I hear you're an expert on cricket.' I said, 'I'm very interested.' He replied in a very stentorian voice, 'We are a rugby school.' I said, 'Oh yes. I don't play rugby.' He said, 'Oh no, you are joking ! You are going to teach

Royal Latin school girls, c. 1965. (P.C.)

rugby.' I said, 'I'm sorry Mr Collis. Nobody asked me if I knew anything about rugby.' He said, 'Let me tell you how to get the boys out to the rugby field.' There followed a ten minute explanation of how to get fifty boys onto the field, then he left me for the whole lesson while he went to see the headmaster to tell him that he had an idiot foisted on him. Since the field was so badly drained that between September and Easter we hardly went out, by which time the cricket season had started.

Leg Beak

Cricket was to be my opportunity to show what I could do. I went out on the first

Fashionable girls from the 1960s relax at Lord's Bridge, Hunter Street. (D.T)

Wednesday afternoon and put down a leg break. This great chap, Les Smith, hoisted into this ball, hitting it so hard, like a rocket. I put my hand up, bang, in goes the ball, snapped a finger and that was the end of my first season.

Every Male Must Do His Duty

Those were the days when every fit male member of staff, under forty-five, took a team each Saturday. I remember the first winter, my uncle died. I told Graham Collis I had to go down to Bournemouth for the funeral. He said, 'You can't do that, you're committed to your team, duty comes first Mr Grimsdale.' I argued with him and he went to the head telling him that I was thinking of not turning up.

George's response was, 'Don't be ridiculous!' Suffice it to say I did my duty as was expected in 1968.

Ed Grimsdale

Above Our Heads

I have many memories of Richardson's paint factory in the 1960s. I worked in the warehouse as a teenager before going to the laboratory after university for a short while. The late 1960s were the age of the mini skirt and I realized why one particular Scotsman spent a long time by the paint blender when I saw him looking up at the spiral staircase that wound down just above his head. Through this door and down these open tread metal stairs came office girls with bonus slips or order queries. Janice, a leggy blonde, made quite a picture tripping down these stairs, though Jock was perhaps less than a gentleman in his enthusiasm. One time the laboratory were experimenting with flecked paint. They chose our canteen wall to test it on while we were eating our sandwiches. There was an almighty crash from just over this wall. Ken 'Shaker' and I had been working there minutes before, making up orders for the Peter Schoen division. When we went back to work we found the partially dismantled heating shaft which had been hanging over our heads all morning had crashed to the floor. If we'd been under it, the large sheet metal tube would have sliced through us both. Those were the days after the railway closed down. Richardson's stored a lot of cardboard in redundant goods sheds near the old railway route. Wilby's coal depot was nearby. Three of us spent an afternoon talking as men did then (before they were new) among the greenery, wild flower smell and insect buzzes of the traditional countryside. We didn't work too hard, it was just too nice a day. There was always plenty of cardboard in the paint factory warehouse. There was a fellow there who used to look after the export packing. He'd built himself a little office area in a corner of the warehouse, using box liners stacked up for walls. He had a thing about Cilla Black and had magazine and newspaper pictures of her cut out and pinned on these walls. I remember one of them showed Cilla in her hot pants. I think he was doing up a cottage for his wife who was ill but she died before they had time to enjoy it together.

Robert Cook

Loco 80041 pulling the 4.18 p.m. to Bletchley, at Buckingham station, 15 February 1956. (R.M.C)

The River

Old Jack Crook the butcher let these old shacks. Joe Dunkley had a bus in there. Jack had used them for slaughtering and had finished with them. I had one and it had a big old copper in it. There was a chap had one opposite and my garage backed on to the river. I went down one morning to get the car to go to Calvert brick works. This policeman was standing there. He asked me if I always kept my car there, he didn't tell me what had happened. I found out afterwards.

Bert Woodfield

Police

I was working on the bridge. The inspector shouted to me 'What are you doing?' Police were all along there. It was a hell of a day. they were looking for the son of the chap who's garage was opposite Bert's garage. They found him by Roper's Farm. He'd wandered through the night and never turned up for work. I suppose he was shocked by what he'd done So was Buckingham. there'd never been a woman's body found in the river before.

Des Tunks

Ivory Tower

George Embleton saw an adviser off the premises with his shotgun and I don't remember seeing another in my first ten years at the Royal Latin School. We were cut off in an ivory tower in North Bucks. After I'd been there for two terms, George set up a boarding house and I became his house master. He invited me over to lunch on Tuesday which was always roast beef day. They had a tremendous cook called Ivy Pickering who lived just opposite the school in Chandos Road and a chap called Timms, from an ancient Bucks gardening family, looking after the gardens at Brookfield. The gardens were walled. All the vegetables were home grown and superbly cooked. I'd always been keen on food and father had an allotment and mother was a very good cook. I thought, as I was cycling in from Thornborough every morning, life in the boarding house was the next best thing, particularly after an embarrassing experience the previous week. I'd found the work tiring. Preparation and marking load is probably greatest in your first year because every lesson is your first. So on this occasion I failed to get up at the appropriate time. Waking up at half past eight, I pulled the curtains back and it was absolutely pouring down and I thought, 'God, I must get to school!' I walked straight downstairs, put on plastic leggings and coat, then straight off to Buckingham. I put my bike against the stone wall, took my plastic leggings down to discover my pyjamas underneath. the only way to save my reputation, considering the whole school was still in assembly, I put my leggings back on and cycled back to Thornborough. Fortunately first lesson was free so no one noticed my absence. I thought I'm not up to looking after myself.

Lonely

Life at the boarding school was rather isolating. There was George, head of this institution and I was his assistant. His wife had quite a gay social life. She was moving up the County circuit, as Mayor of Buckingham and onto the County Council. George accompanied her rather like Dennis Thatcher followed Margaret. So one term I was on duty every night every week from September to Christmas. I never left the campus. I didn't notice because it was such fun. I was young. When George got back in the evening he called me in for a few glasses of scotch and would have happily talked the night away. He was a great raconteur. Sometimes I was totally incapable of teaching the next morning but I didn't worry, I'd cheered him up. I think he was lonely. He wasn't part of the county set. He'd rather talk about his World War Two exploits in the navy than attend a champagne party.

Monastic

I hadn't really discovered women by that time and living in a monastic boys boarding house set me back. It was fortuitous that a young lady came on to the campus and, with

Royal Latin School staff cricket team 1981, Skipper Ed Grimsdale, front row with bat. (E.G.)

nowhere to live, was given a flat under the clock tower next to the boarding house. I suppose she was the first woman I'd met in four years and we started going out and eventually married.

Chop Off My Head

It was a good life in the boarding house. We had up to fifty boys, all fed and watered. All my money was pocket money. Home-sickness was the biggest problem for the boarders. George had a social conscience, so ten percent were from problem families. I recall one boy, let's call him Andrew. He was perhaps the brightest boy I've ever met, extremely good at chemistry. I don't know what his problems were but he came into the third form halfway through the year. I taught him but you could not relate to him as a person. Every summer we used to have a camp at Silverstone and the boys thought, 'Here's an odd ball.' One night they took him and dragged him through silage. He absolutely stank. He said, 'I'm in a mess.' He had no other clothes so I told him to stay in his tent in the morning, then wash and dry his gear while I went off with the lads in the morning. Half way through the morning I came back to inspect the lunch. We had large billycans on a fire, one full of carrots, one mince and one potatoes. I lifted the lid off the potatoes and there were his underpants. I lifted the lid of the carrots and there were his trousers gently brewing away. The other pot contained his shirt. I admit I shouted a bit roughly, calling him to come out. He said, 'I can't come here because I haven't any clothes on.' Eventually he crawled out of his tent on all fours. I was beside the fire, near a very large axe we used to chop wood for the camp fire. As he crept toward me he jumped on the axe,

picked it up and went to chop off my head. I think he would have succeeded if the head boy had not appeared to grab it. He was sent back to the boarding house in disgrace to be shipped on his way at the end of term.

Young Matron

My next memory is from a few nights later. We had a very young matron and she had a fairly gay time with the lads. She slept in the room above mine. Mine was at the end of the corridor on the ground floor. At about three in the morning I was woken by this blood curdling scream which was so loud I thought I'd made it in my sleep. Pulling myself together, I realized it was real and sat up shaking. The staircase was opposite my door and when I opened it, at the top of the stairs I saw a woman covered in blood and I screamed. Matron's voice answered fairly normally, 'For heaven's sake Ed what are you screaming about? It's me. Yes, something nasty has happened.' Then I realized she was dressed from head to foot in a blood red night robe, of course I'd never seen her like this. She said she'd woken up with one of the boys on top of her trying to rape her.

Mirror Test

What do you do at that time in a boarding house full of fifty boys? I had to get hold of George. I knew his house well, but not where he slept so I went in shouting, 'George, George, Mr Embleton.' When I found him he said, 'Oh what, what, God, somebody's tried to rape matron. Bloody hell! Let's get the bugger, let's get the bugger.' I said, 'We've got a

Floods again, Nelson Street, Barry Tomkins and son Craig enjoy an opportunity for water sport outside the paint factory spring, c. 1972. (J.S.)

problem, everybody's now in bed.' 'We'll try the mirror test, yeh, we'll get Edna's mirror and we'll hold it in front of them and the one that's been panting will mist it up.' So we went from boy to boy but it didn't work. I can't remember how we discovered it was Andrew who had done it. He was very disturbed. We heard a year later he had the job of baby-sitting a young girl, raping her while the mother was out and going to jail. Many of the problem kids we did proud but they made life hairy.

Girls

When I moved in, the girls' boarding house had just started in an annexe, before Rotherfield House – a manor house – was converted to accommodate fifty girls at the opposite end of the campus. Things were strict, the idea was 'no sex please we're British'. But boys were in charge of locking up the school at night and there'd often be a window left open for the boys to climb out of Brookfield and the girls to climb out of Rotherfield. They would often meet in matron's room in the main block. Where there was a bed.

First Time Club

One of the boys came back and said, 'We used to have a library first time club, sir. That was for pupils who'd first had sex during preparation in the library. Did you know?' 'I said, 'No.' I only ever caught one couple in there and we had this rule that if a boy and girl came closer than nine inches they would be punished. We always assumed it was the boys not the girls fault. But however hard you try, nature finds a way.

Discipline

George drew on his wartime experience and was a great believer in naval discipline. The girls' boarding school was not such a success because unlike boys they weren't so happy with spartan conditions. Beds were iron, each pupil had one yard of carpet at his bedside, the rest of the floor was bare. Boys had no wardrobes except for a central one where all the suits and uniforms were hung.

Every boy had two hangers on an open rail in the dormitory and each had a locker one metre square. They had virtually no private life, living in public as if it were a public school. We set up the girls boarding house on similar lines but I think girls needed more home comforts and the house never really took off. We had matrons, who were fearsome creatures, some ex-forces. I remember Mrs McKay who said, 'I eat people like you, Mr Grimsdale, for breakfast.' She ran a regime of terror. For example, if you did not eat your food it was recycled. In one case it went too far, when the cooks prepared some scones for the girl boarders and one girl tried to eat one. They were very bitter. So matron said, 'Right, they'll have them again for supper,' and they came back the next day for tea. To make them palatable they'd cut them in two and poured blackcurrant jam on to each half.

Ed Grimsdale outside Brookfield House, Summer 2000.

When the girls came to eat them the jam was a sort of florescent green. Someone went screaming out of the boarding house, coming over to me in the boys' boarding house with the magnificent dripping scones. 'Matron has poisoned us, Sir. You're a chemist, what's happening?' She pleaded. I said, 'Let's go to the chemistry lab.' I had a shrewd idea that this was a jam that had changed colour due to alcohol or acid levels. I tested it, finding it very alkaline whereas jam would have been acid. The scones were very hard suggesting use of much bicarbonate of soda. The cooks must have run out of flour and used this as a substitute. When matron added blackcurrant jam they turned it a violent green. Matron hadn't poisoned them, she'd just been dead set on recycling; which was typical of her.

Nicely Green

My wife became girls' dormitory mistress and was required to eat roast pork which had a green patina on it. This was pork which had been fed to the girls the previous week and they hadn't eaten it. So nicely green, it was warmed up and served up again!

Edna's Parties

Finances for both the boarding houses were amalgamated. Our way of life in the boys' house was magnificent but meant not giving too much money to the girls. You also had to feed Edna, the head's wife who had this great social life and if a party was required it came out of the boys' kitchen. The Needle and Thread Club was a very old established club, raising funds by selling cakes. Edna said, 'No problem, we'll make some cakes.' So every single ounce of flour and sugar in the boys' boarding house was used to make cakes to raise money for the church and so on. We were feeding part of North Bucks, wining and dining them on a grandiose scale.

Lavish Hospitality

The University of Buckingham was set up, originally, for a meeting in the front drawing room of Brookfield house. We were able to offer lavish hospitality. The girls' boarding school suffered a shortage of funds to balance the books at the end of the month.

Not Acceptable!

In those days it wasn't acceptable for girls to smoke and the boys went behind the bicycle shed. George Embleton was always very keen on shooting and knew the boarding house had been a hunting, fishing and shooting lodge in the nineteenth century. He had a gun ready to shoot rabbits. I remember this Saturday about 7 a.m., I got up and it was a bright sunny morning. I was looking across the lawn toward the shrubbery which was at the top of the railway line. Suddenly George comes out of his house, across the lawn with his gun, 'Bang! Bang!' Straight into the bushes he fired, obviously aiming for a rabbit and out sprang a boy boarder. Curiously he was called Andrew Doe! The boy was shouting, 'Don't shoot me sir, it's me sir.' 'Er, you

Mrs Stanton with Cubs and Brownies, early 1970s. (D.T.)

deserve it boy, you were smoking!' George roared, I nearly had yer there, I nearly had yer.' But I don't know who was more frightened. George was an appalling shot and could well have bagged Andrew.

Lunatic

George was a great character but he did some lunatic things. He was probably the only head in the county who would say in 1970 that pupils wore indoor and outdoor shoes and we had about five blocks. They had to change on entering and exiting each. His rule was carried out with a rod of iron. Not a lot of people would have had the character to make such rules work. He put heart and soul into the school, he'd be in his room typing memos into the night. It was all manual, no word processor and he had a curious turn of phrase, 'please to do this', or 'please to do that'. He loved gardening and planted some unusual specimens of trees in the ground. He also liked a good edge to his lawns and would be out there all hours getting it right and squirting poisons. If the weather was hot he'd be stripped to his underpants, looking like a derelict in long yellowy underpants and happily edging his lawns. When my wife came for a teaching job in 1973, the first person she met when she entered the grounds was George, dressed like this and she thought he was the eccentric gardener. introducing herself, she said, 'Will you take me to the head teacher?' Indignantly, he said, 'I am the headmaster of this school!' He was extremely independent minded.

Cut Up A Body!

We had an eccentric English teacher, let's call him Bob. He had two old cars parked at the school and spent much of his spare time taking them to bits. He didn't seem to have anywhere to live, so we gave him a room in the boarding house. I was called to his bedroom one morning because the cleaner said, 'There's blood coming from his chest of drawers, I think he's cut up a body!' I opened the drawer and there were many glasses of red wine, about two dozen. It transpired he was alcoholic and poured them ready in case he woke up in the night and on this occasion he'd not noticed that he had knocked one over, leaving it dripping like blood. Poor chap was asked to leave and died within the year. But he was the greatest English teacher I've known, making Shakespeare come alive to the least interested.

Ed Grimsdale

Local girls, Mitre Street, evocative of early 1960s innocence. (G.W.)

95

Ed Grimsdale, teaching chemistry, Royal Latin school, c. 1980. (E.G.)

Better Looked After

My father died when I was fourteen. The teachers at the Latin school were really supportive. I think we were probably better looked after than today's school children. George Embleton had a difficult job and demanded high standards. Headmasters are always figures of fun, but I thought he ran a good school. We tiptoed past his study which showed his discipline worked. They wore gowns which was strange at first, coming as I did from a little village school in the 1950s. The old Latin school in Chandos road wasn't much bigger than the one I'd left. Though it was cramped, it eased the way when we moved to the new school which was very big.

Pat Chisholme

Winkle Pickers

In the 1960s the Air Training Corps was based in a hut in the grounds of the old Royal Latin School and was mainly involved the grammar school's pupils. It was like an annex, like the public schools had the Combined Cadet Force, the Latin school had the ATC. My father died when I was eleven so we couldn't afford for me to have more than one pair of shoes. Mine were patent leather winkle pickers which combined with my longer than average blonde hair, made me a target for criticism on the parade ground! I remember marching with the squadron, wheeling into Chandos Road from London Road. Near the cinema were a gaggle of sneering chanting yobs, advising us in a parody of an NCO, 'Up, two, three four' there might still have been the rump of an empire but Air Training Corps was not cool in the Swinging Sixties. I didn't mind because I lived in a *Boy's Own* world of wartime heroes and imperial greatness. I wanted to be a fighter pilot until I got to university where comfortable students were protesting against the evils of empire and the Vietnam War. That changed me. The wider world was much less certain than the one I'd grown up in. I felt guilty about my simple ambition.

Robert Cook

Little Emperors

Trade unions became more important in the 1960s, as time and motion study became part of the paint factory routine. Mr Airey was absolute God at the factory. We made paint for a Dutch company called Peter Schoen. We were like little emperors, all getting along in our empire. Then Beaver's took us over. In 1973 I looked around and thought the world was bigger than Richardson's and considered starting my own business. Food, clothing and transport are the basic industries and I chose the latter after dabbling a bit in all three. We started off as car and private hire. It grew and when the university came in 1976 a whole new world opened up.

Alan Britton

The old building line along to the Whale before demolition put Woolworth's in place in March 1964. Summer 1960 and this Military Load, a Bristol Helicopter, hauled by a Scammell recovery tractor, stops for a cuppa on market hill. Small boys are excited and a girl behind the Red Rover bus shows a restrained interest. (I.B.)

Peter Tunks adopts a cool image, early 1970s. (D.T.)

Come And See Me

When I went to live at Radclive, Michael Richardson came up to me and said if you want to change anything around here come and see me. I am the Godfather of Radclive. You'd be pulled into his study in the mill and be plied with appalling red wine which he bought in bulk from France and offered one of his cancerous cigars. He was one of the last of the great pirate kings!

Clive Birch MBE

Never Said

I've met some interesting people in the course of my private hire work. Arthur Lowe used to visit Stowe school concerts because his stepson was music master there. He and his wife stayed at the White Hart Hotel. Arthur was a lovely man rather like his screen self. His wife was a bit of a tartar. He was her second husband. I've carried several well known people and never made a fuss. Then Arthur Lowe 's wife said to me once, 'You know who we are?' I said, 'Yes'. She said, 'Only you never said anything'. I said, 'I thought you'd be glad I hadn't.' For some reason that seemed to strike a spark with Arthur because he began to talk about things. I remember we stopped at a pub once. He used to wear a deerstalker hat, like Sherlock Holmes, and in a pub he'd always sit with his back to everybody in an alcove.

Alan Britton

CHAPTER 5

Modern Times

Stirling Moss fills her up at Ganderton's Garage en route to nearby Silverstone in 1960. Young John is proud to do the honours. Courtesy R.H. Chapman (J.G.)

Class Issue

I had fantastic teachers at Buckingham Secondary School but the school was poorly funded. I remember Mr Neave. I'd give him a top award. The teachers really gave support. Only recently have they got the money they needed. All the girls I went to school with did well and I know girls who went to the Royal Latin School who thought they were better and ended up in little council houses with three children and no aspirations. I don't think there's any point in having two schools, it has caused

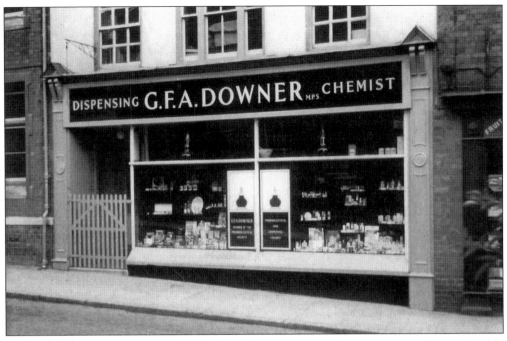

Seaton's shop front, c. 1960. (I.B.)

friction. Secondary Modern School children can feel let down by the system. There's very, much a 'them and us' attitude. It's noticeable. Latin School pupils tend to have a very different upbringing to the secondary modern. There's definitely a class issue.

Paula Wilkes

Overstated

The retail centre, within a largely surviving period townscape went through rapid decline of service shops – butchers, greengrocers, ironmongers etc. – but started to recover with boutiques, restaurants and fancy goods outlets. old property was redeveloped, and there is no doubt the university, helped, bringing student spending power, substantial renovation of peripheral streetscapes and adding to a new sense of pride – though it must be said that the social input of staff, students and institution has been overstated. With rail electrification, the M40 and a poorly developed road structure, Buckingham nonetheless found itself across roads, albeit one that was little more than a lunch stop, if that. It gradually became on the way to everywhere and was by passed.

Clive Birch MBE

Head Butt

Boys still have to learn to be boys whatever the do-gooders and feminists might say. So I suppose the youth football league is a good way of doing this. My son played for some years for Preston Gawcott. I suppose it's always been a rough game but I was amazed by the foul language of some parents and bemused by one mum from an opposing team. Her goalkeeper son was sent off for leaving his area during a so-called friendly. They were one of the self consciously elite teams and the mum couldn't handle this indignity. She burst into tears bordering on the hysterical. I fear some might be living out failed personal ambitions. My son has been head butted and kicked many times. It's no wonder we have such a hopeless national team considering the grass roots. Youngsters see such bad examples. I must say Preston Gawcott's own standards are impeccable but these days it seems to pay to cheat at anything if you've a mind set on fortune.

A parent

Character

Buckingham has lost its character. As a young girl and when I first married there were a lot of old shops. Most of the shopkeepers would remark when you were a young mother, that they remembered you as a child. The old shops like Cantell's and the Chocolate Box, used to fascinate my son when he was small. That'sall gone now.

Sheila Wilkes (née Wilby)

Tradition And Change

Buckingham had to change. The town centre architecture was compromised in the early 1970s. There were some lovely old

Seaton's shop front, c. 1960. (I.B.)

George Walden, in centre, during the winter of 1987's election campaign trail. (R.C.)

shops pulled down. Just to have change isn't positive, neither is hanging on to the past. You want pockets of history. It's a mixed bag. I remember childhood days, passing Vyle's shop in Castle street. It was a big department shop. There's nothing like it now. As a child I knew nothing about the world. People didn't used to travel so much in those days. But I think the future of Buckingham is very positive. It's what you make of it. I value my membership of the town council. I'm also a District Councillor and it helps me to represent the people's view, not mine. Traditions are important but you must allow for different approaches. There was a problem at the last mayor making ceremony; leading Cllr Cockerton to resign. I thought having the school children singing was a breath of fresh air. But Cllr Cockerton heard people criticising the organisation, hearing comments about there being no one to meet the mayor's guests. Cllr Cockerton chose to resign, I thought it was enough to debate it. As a result we've found a method for mayor making ceremonies with scope for individual imprint.

Derek Isham

Colour

Wimbledon was the first thing I saw on a colour 625, in 1967. I've always been like a little boy with TV and radio but I think television has killed a lot of the everyday life in many homes. You can't talk with it blaring out. It's on for too many hours. They

April 2000. Meadow Walk shopping centre and this lone piper contrasts with the black watch who piped here for the Queen Mother and public in June 1963. (R.J.C.)

can't fill the slots with good quality programmes. You don't get the little bright bits on the news anymore.

Ian Beckett

Very Depressing

TV news can be very depressing if you're a bit low. I know a lot of people who don't bother to watch it.

Des Tunks

Times Change

I used to go to go to the Chandos after work at the paint factory. I particularly remember seeing D.H. Lawrence's *Women in Love*. I was very interested in D.H. Lawrence and this was a shocking film for its day, based on one of his books. I remember sitting in the warehouse on a pallet load of paint t reading Lawrence's Literary criticism. I was a romantic teenager secretly in love with Janice, a blonde secretary girl who looked good in her miniskirts; I would never dare ask her out. As I read my romantic book, Barney an earthy Irishman asked me what it was about. When I explained its romantic content, he laughed mockingly and declared, 'B******s! It's just in with the pr****!' I felt very disillusioned. At the time I felt there must be more to sex and procreation than that. Those were hippy days, when long haired blokes like me used to have to put up with the mockery that you couldn't tell us from the girls. Times change. I was at a Latin School parents' evening recently and saw lots of girls I could hardly tell from boys. But that's a dangerous thing to say. There's not the freedom of expression anymore. Our leaders have their special goals and we must give way to the needs of political correctness and social engineering.

Robert Cook

Strange

When I came to Buckingham there was one car in Gawcott Road. Now you can't park at all. I was looked on as a newcomer with my strange accent. Now there are so many new people.

Dandy Robinson

Change

It's better in some ways. Perhaps older people don't think so, probably the younger ones do. If we talk to youngsters it goes in one ear and out the other. they think you're romancing. they don't want to know. It's a different life to when we were twenty.

Bert Woodfield

Same Boat

We were all in the same boat. In the old days if there was trouble down North End Square it was mostly drink related. These days if they're drunk they're really drunk!

Des Tunks

Where Will it End?

In the village just before and after the war there were only three or four car owners, now it seems nearly every house has three or four cars. We now travel more by car in a year than our grandfathers travelled in a year. They've opened up the whole country to the ordinary person. I don't know where it will stop.

Joe Pallett

Des Tunks taking great care while working at precision engineering firm Hartridge in Tingewick Road, early 1970s. (D.T.)

Bruce Jarvis at his Station Terrace Garage, March 1999. The former brewery was used as accomodation by 1930s hunger marchers. The site is now advertsied for development but Des Tunks said it should be preserved as a historic site. Bruce says that he must think of his family's future after years of hard work. (R.J.C.)

Mentality

But there is a new mentality with people coming in saying Buckingham needs this or that, we'll sort it out. There are people who want to hang on to Buckingham as we knew it. When I came here it hadn't changed much since the turn of the century. People still stood up for *God Save the Queen* at the Chandos.

Alan Britton

Character

The character of Buckingham is bound to change, you can't stop it. Bill Markham and I meet for a couple of hours in the pub each week. We're always talking about thirty or forty years ago, it makes you feel old. I've never regretted coming here from Southampton, all my children grew up and were educated here. They're solid citizens. It depends what sort of life you're looking for. I like peace and quiet, the easy way and Buckingham has been good for that. It's a place where you can be yourself with no pretensions.

Moving In

When I came to Buckingham in 1968 it was a very sleepy, parochial, and rural. there isn't that feeling at the Royal Latin School now. Many of our pupils come from Milton Keynes. It's a pity our local government isn't more like Milton Keynes. A unitary authority keeps the lines of communication clearer and keeps democracy closer to the people. I'm particularly concerned about planning because Aylesbury Vale are so remote and there's tremendous scope for corruption once there is outline planning permission. If you're a lucky landowner in this area you become a multi-millionaire overnight. People in authority can make some very poor and others very rich. I'd prefer Buckingham to be separate rather than be developed and swallowed into other conurbations. What matters to me is a feeling of place. Otherwise there is no purpose to travel if everywhere is roughly the same. People moving into the district with a lot of economic resources have the effect of pushing up house prices beyond the pockets of local people, perhaps those formerly employed in declining agriculture. There's a possibility we might dilute what it is to be Buckingham. It is very difficult to sustain the farming community, it's a terrible time for farmers generally. The quality of the local paper is a cause for concern. There's not the controversy in the letters page. People don't care on the whole. Many don't turn out for elections. I think it's vital to be involved. Something needs to be done to encourage real democracy and make people care. I think most of southern England will become a concrete jungle and we will lose most of our agriculture. The distance between towns is shrinking.

Ed Grimsdale

Proud Of Our Roots

Among earlier newcomers was a young councillor, Chris Fogden. I believe Buckingham owes more to him than most.

The new indoor swimming and fitness complex under construction, August 1995.

Castle House displays the majesty of Buckingham.

He was mayor for three years, during which time he either instigated or saw through the relief road, the community centre and industrial park. Then revived the chamber of trade. Others I recall are the Whiteheads, organic farmers long before it was fashionable, the Wheelers whose land now boasts a splendid stable complex between Stowe and Silverstone and major plant hire outfit. To be in the middle of a field and hear Steve Wheeler berating a driver who is not where he should be is to witness a masterpiece of polite invective and succinct direction. As his father Bob, retired now and a former County Councillor, observed, all the Wheelers are long in body and short in leg. They are also strong in mind and spirit, the sort of people who supply the bedrock of a local community, because they are proud of their roots, know everyone and care. There are many more. There was MP George Walden lording it intellectually, and Aylesbury Vale's Chairman Colonel quietly serving Buckingham when everyone thought he was above it all. The Hobdays came and went at the town hall – and that's another story! Derek Edmondson was a banker who restored Castle House, and made his own mouldings, turned his own timbers and laid his own bricks.

Clive Birch MBE

Tesco Bags

I always feel, being in Buckingham I've met a lot of interesting people. I was amazed at the number of Sirs, Lords and Ladies. I think it was partly due to the war. A lot of old colonials came back to England and for some reason they surfaced around here. Miss Keys from Tingewick was from one of the few families with two VCs. Her father was Admiral Keys of the Mediterranean fleet. She was eccentric, wearing Tesco bags on her feet as protection against water when she was out walking, and talking to me about great events in a matter of fact way. She wore a brooch given to her by the Queen of Belgium. Her father got his VC at Jutland and her brother while trying to capture Rommel, I think. They were the kind of people who either won a VC or ended up dead. They're a dying breed. Buckingham is filling up with newcomers but it all seems bland to me.

Alan Britton.

Rush

It was so slow when I came to Buckingham. Nobody ran. Londoners tear about. Now it's all rush here and I don't go back to London because there are so few Londoners left, it's all foreigners.

Dandy Robinson

What A Lady!

When I first came to Buckingham I was told that if I wanted anything done, I had to convince two people – Mary McManus and Edna Embleton. They ran Buckingham, they said. In the event, I never knew Mary well, but Edna became a close friend. She was effectively 'Lady Buckingham.' The first time we met, I was pontificating at the Franciscan Building, when I heard this voice 'What's he know about it? He's only been here five minutes' And she was right. We never looked back. I served under her

Those were the days when large lorries had no choice but to clog the narrow town streets.

Tesco superstore, July 1999, built on part of the old Wipac site and open twenty-four hours a day.

chairmanship of the Latin School governors, and she under mine in the Heritage Trust. What a worker, what a character, and what an effective lady. Edna saved the hospital, of that I have no doubt. she entrenched a sense of tradition in the town council, and she raised squillions, much of it for the Old Gaol project. I really miss her.

Clive Birch MBE

Not Far

Videos helped finish our cinema. people were content to stay home and watch TV and youngsters wanted to go to Milton Keynes. It's not far. As for the town, I think it has gone to pot. Trades people pay high rates and people shop at Tesco. The University students don't integrate because they're on a two year crash course and haven't time. But they've brought prosperity with all the property renovation.

Gwen Harris (née Parker)

Gravity

When you get a facility as big as Tesco on the edge of town, you shift the centre of gravity away from local shops. Tesco is a fine place to shop for people with cars but if you live the other side of the Brackley road without one, divisive. The Heartland's scheme was meant to involve removing an old bridge which was an eyesore. No one seemed to know what it was there for. Men came to knock it down and suddenly sewage spilled out because it was there to carry it across the river. The local authority said it carried a rising main. The bridge is still there. Planning is undemocratic. Developers have large profit margins and conditions are ignored with no action taken. Because you have several layers of local government you can have housing development ahead of infrastructure. Schooling problems are exacerbated because parents are free to choose where their children go. The Royal Latin School takes about 400 students from outside the area, so we have 400 spare places whereas the secondary school probably needs 400 places. Winslow would be better off as part of Milton Keynes rather than rely on Buckingham for its schools. As soon as it's on the east-west rail link there'll be an explosion of people. The railway corridor will attract factory units and more people who want to live there. These new people will see themselves as a suburb of Milton Keynes. I don't think that will happen to Buckingham. We are helped by our history. We glory in our separateness, but I think Winslow has been sold down the railway line to Milton Keynes. I was born in an era of debate. I love criticising. I hate consensus, I see it ruling us.

Ed Grimsdale

Open all hours. Advert for Tesco superstore just off the London Road roundabout August 2000. (R.J.C)

Heartlands development, September 1998, viewed from the old bridge.

Shalln't Shift

There was a radio dealer opposite the builders where I worked in the 1930s. They had one of the new fangled Baird televisions in the window. It was quite something. I watch the news now and a bit of the soap operas, but for comedy I stick to Ronnie Barker and *Dad's Army*. I don't like modern music. I like Glen Miller, that sort of thing. I shalln't shift from that.

F.R. Markham

Rotten Borough

The University has helped the Old Gaolers with their heritage work. The Royal Latin School is another centre of excellence and we have a lot of live culture. But we could do with a late night bus service so that our kids could get out to use facilities further afield. There's a lot here for the middle classes. I've sat on the Crime Prevention panel. Friday and Saturday nights are problems. We don't seem to able to educate our young against drinking to excess. The grammar school debate has been going on since the 1970s. The government is out to weaken resistance in areas like Buckingham. For the last 200 years the town has been a kind of rotten borough, but it has its own identity. I don't see an immediate threat to our grammar school.

Ed Grimsdale

Very African

Chief Ogon, a Nigerian Minister came to the university. I first met him when he pulled up in a white Rolls Royce and knocked my door. He said he'd been told to call on me for transport, accommodation, schools and doctor. I said I thought he'd been given the wrong address. He had a list of doctors, schools etc. Taking £1,000 from his pocket, he threw it on the settee. My wife was amazed. Then he slung his coat around his shoulders and said, 'Pick me up at the Waverley Hotel in Banbury tomorrow.' That's how it started. Over time I found accommodation at a farm near Preston Bissett and his family came over. I suppose he was about thirty-six and for around five years I was absorbed in Nigerian culture, looking after him all the time. He had children all over the country and was at the university himself. He didn't have a European nuance, he was very 'African' and looked to me to put him right.

Alan Britton

How It's Got

I knew everyone in the village, but as I go down now, to the post office to get my little bit of pension, I might see half a dozen people and don't know anyone at all. That's how it's got in the villages now.

Stan Beckett

Important To Share

My uncle Mr Evenson died in 1961 and I took over running the business. I'd been married ten years then. My wife and I got on very well. I'm a widower, but if I had the chance I would marry again. It's

The infamous 105ft long blue bridge, being delivered from Coalville in Leicestershire to the Heartlands Development, pauses by the Grand Junction pub on 23 January 1999. The bridge had to be jacked higher on the trailer to clear the High Street's railings that were obstructing the turn. (B.W.A.) (Jake McNulty)

Family life, Bath Lane Terrace, mid 1950s and Des Tunks' grandmother, Florence Balinger enjoys a laugh with Aunt Gladys Cummins. (D.T.)

important to share your life.

The Town It Was

Buckingham isn't the town it was. Western Avenue, where I live, Bourtonville and Westfields, had been completed before the war but not Page Hill, Linden Village or Badgers. The population was only about 3,500 when I came, now it must be nearly 15,000. You can't run a business like I used to today. The property was vast, running from the Market Square right down to the river. To keep that warehouse full of stock would cost too much nowadays I inherited it from my uncle and his brother came here to live. We formed a Limited Company. I became Chairman when Mr Evenson's brother died in 1977. We closed the business on 1 March 1986. We couldn't keep up with businesses like B&Q. They didn't have to maintain accounts and ledgers. All our farmers, builders and tradesmen had accounts. So did a lot of the private houses. We were busy right up to the end. I had it valued and was told my property was worth more than the business. I sold to a developer. It's now the Victoria Wine Company and the back is luxury flats. I wasn't sad. I was ready to retire and my wife wanted me to. I feel something when I see the shop, but sentiment is on the wane. I'm eighty-two and have plenty to do looking after myself.

F.R. Markham

Pool

Money was raised to build something to commemorate service people's effort in the war. Most wanted a maternity wing built on the hospital but they built the open air swimming pool Now that's gone there's nothing to remind us.

Des Tunks

Community Spirit

Buckingham has developed a lot since I came here in 1974. We've got to be careful or we may lose this great community spirit. Coming from London, I thought it was wonderful, people were so involved with each other. I know these days some just treat it as a place to live and only know their house. When I first came here there were just a few little shops. I still feel something has been lost. The quality is not the same. Shopkeepers are more inclined to treat you as just a customer, rather than an individual. Tesco's is no good without transport. Thank goodness we've still got Budgen's. There are a lot of older people here.

Hospital

I was on the community health council, visiting dozens of surgeries throughout the

Des and Edna Tunks prepare to leave their life long marital home in Station Terrace, November 2000 as the developers move closer – the garden once accommodating Des's Aviary is now itself being developed as the pressure to expand Buckingham is unabated.

Gillian Wain, centre, and friends play on her dad's tractor, early 1950s. The field has now been developed as part of the county expansion plan and named Wain Close. (G.W.)

Vale. I am aware how well off we are and really must retain our cottage hospital.

Peggy Dale

Time Was Different

Chief Ogon had a permanent suite at the Green Hotel and we used to go down to meet people like Tiny Rowlands, Julian Amery and General Goan who'd been to Warwick University. African students looked to him, as they did at home, for help with money problems. he was Chief. Every day we drew £1,000 from the bank and he would stop in the square where students would tell him their worries. The farm became a sort of transit camp for Nigerians

and I used to walk around with money stuck in various pockets. My wife and I became like an aunt and uncle, but it was hard work mentally. I felt his outlook as an African was different. Time did not seem to mean the same to him. We might be halfway to Gatwick airport and he'd decide to come back. Sadly the last I heard of him was that he'd been arrested and died in gaol during a period of internal strife.

Picked Up

Drugs were a problem on air routes to Nigeria. I was waiting for people at Gatwick. I had the contract for Charmendean School. All the children there belonged to overseas people, military and diplomatic wireless people who were abroad. We used to take these people back and forth to the airport and pick up new ones and I was there to collect Nigerians. About an hour after the plane had landed there was no sign of the children. I was used to that because they used to come over with minders, nannies or whatever. I saw a Nigerian lady coming out and asked her if she was off the flight I was meeting. 'Yes,' she said, 'Were there any children on it?' 'Yes, I'll go back and see if I can find them.' I walked back toward the customs barrier and as we got there a man in a white suit came through and she spoke to him. The next minute we were surrounded by people who turned out to be police. It turned out this man had been fingered, probably before he left and it was a case of see who he meets. It took me a lot of explaining and I refused to be taken behind closed doors to do it. I don't know what happened to the man in the white suit.

Alan Britton

Intermarriage

There used to be a lot of intermarriage, people were very much related to each other. People said I'd never be accepted because I was very much an outsider but I got very involved, really getting to know people joining the town council in 1978 and becoming mayor in 1986. As a district councillor whenever I got up others would say, 'Oh, she's always

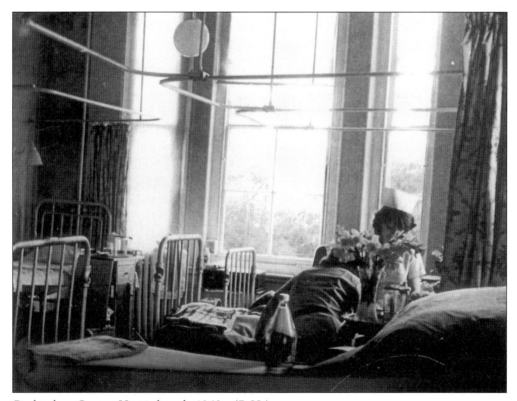

Buckingham Cottage Hospital, early 1960s. (B.H.)

Man in braces, veteran car salesman Henry Thomas at the former Phillips Motor works in Chandos Road. Times change but Henry keeps selling cars with his unique style!

complaining about something in Buckingham,' but you had to make them listen to our needs. Talking to local kids, I realise there's no where for them to go, no dance halls. So they go to the pubs and do silly things. For years we've tried to get Project Street Life going and it's proving successful.

High Regard

There's little trouble here compared to other towns and we're very fortunate with our schools The nicest thing about the town is that people care for each other. I'm so pleased Buckingham University has established here because it exerts

such a pull for Buckingham abroad. I've been fortunate to serve on the friends committee and was at the ceremony where Sir Dennis received his diploma. I have a high regard for Margaret Thatcher. She's quite short but her manner of speaking can be quite intimidating. She'd look you straight in the eye and could put you quite in awe.

Peggy Dale

Still Charming

Many think Buckingham is still charming but for me it has lost the original charm it had for me, but those who come here now must still see something different. the University made a difference, it had a big effect, giving the town a bit of status after Milton Keynes looked like turning it into a dormitory town. A lot of good quality housing has been built for middle and upper management types. Buckingham has been seen as a snobbish place. The population was 4,000 when I came. It must be 12-13,000. I think the expansion target is 17,000. That's four times larger than when I came here, so it's bound to change.

Alan Britton

Tough Act

George Embleton was headmaster from 1948 to 78 and was a tough act to follow. When he arrived the school was a mess, when he left it was very sad. It had been very much a one man show and he didn't want to leave. Brookfield had been his and Edna's home and he was beginning to suffer from Alzheimer's disease. He was suffering from delusions and was not happy that somebody else was moving into his house. So when he left he turned off the water and electricity. Nothing was functioning. That did my career the power of good because I was here in the summer holidays as resident boarding house master and was the only person who knew where everything was. I turned it all back on for the new head and within a term I became Senior Teacher on the back of it. It was all because I gave the punctiliously clean headmaster, Peter Luff, his first bath!

The Flosh and Lord's Bridge. (D.T.)

Baroness Thatcher receives an export award from Lord Lieutenant of Bucks, John Freemantle, 1994 under the watchful eye of University Vice Chancellor Sir Richard Luce. Baroness Thatcher was made university Chancellor in 1992. Buckingham & Winslow Advertiser.

Mimicry

Peter Luff had a characteristic soft shoe shuffle along the corridor and boys are very good at mimicry. They nick named him 'Penguin' straight away. I was 'Grimmy'. They usually captured the essence of a person. The head of games was called 'Boris the Spider' because he was bald with about twenty hairs sticking out! His head looked like a large spider. In Christmas reviews the pupils would pin you down with frightening accuracy, though they don't do that quite so much these days. I think kids' experiences are much broader in life these days. The role of the teacher as a figure in their lives has diminished. They don't seem to have quite the same need to take us to bits. Teachers wouldn't be happy to turn out as we did, to take Saturday morning teams and the kids spend less time at school. the academic drive is more effective and results better but we have lost a sense of balance. Pupils achieve very well on a narrow front but don't come out educated people.

Ed Grimsdale

Worry About the Boys

Girls are more fussy and the GCSE system and national curriculum suits them. Our greatest failures in school are bright boys who are switched off. Achieving eight to nine GCSEs is not necessarily an indicator of ability at A'level. The system militates against bright boys who doubt it. Much of the work is continuous assessment. I worry about the boys. Education these days can be a very demeaning experience. It is processing kids in a very primitive fashion. I actually enjoy the excitement of making better thinkers and cricketers, not processing people. The new generation of teachers are supremely efficient at this new process. I hate having a set order of teaching. Learning is far more organic, a meeting of minds.

Get A Job

The majority of kids want to know how what they do at school is going to help them get a job I want to reverse that culture. It doesn't matter what you teach, it's how you teach it.

Laws

Teachers are no longer laws unto themselves with National Curriculum and OFSTED awarding funding for improvement. Your

Buckingham Youths enjoying all the fun of the fair, October 1999.

Buckingham Fair, 1999, and a rather alert baby studies the prizes on offer. Prizes and surprizes are the order of the day now!

scheme of work is not your own, it's set out in tablets of stone. You have your head of department breathing down your neck, inspecting you once a term and his line manager is inspecting him. There's very little freedom left. We're attracting a different sort of teacher. I'm taking early retirement, partly because I want a degree of freedom that is no longer there. I'm no longer interested in the A'level I'm teaching. Much of it is redundant and boring. The interesting bits have to be left out because increasingly I must keep rigidly to the syllabus and I'll be criticized by parents for departing from it. I was the type of teacher who'd say we'll do this because it's interesting and they'd learn by osmosis. I find increasingly I'm teaching things I don't

believe has value for the individual. I feel like a machine turning out results. I feel that tension. I'm losing heart really. I started teaching at a time when you could engage with young minds and inspire. There's little opportunity for that now. Management overwhelms my life as deputy head. I must do many things I actually think are wrong. the nature of the teaching experience has changed and the nature of education has changed. It was fun, 90 % of the job I came for was fun, making the other 10% worth it. The scope for teachers to be idealistic and off the wall is reduced and the pupils receive less. They have people who are cautious looking over their shoulders. they don't reach the heights or the depths. I've given some awful lessons but occasionally lessons pupils don't forget. Those coming into teaching in the 1950s and 1960s generally brought culture and could engage on a wide front. that is not expected or given now. My job is to manage and make sure only that required is done. I've lost my cause.

Female Outlook

When I started teaching boys loved to smoke and girls didn't. Now it's a girl problem, I think it's a slimming device and it's cool to smoke. The Royal Latin School used to be male centred with books about the achievements of men and three-quarters of the staff male. Now out of sixty-five staff fewer than twenty are male and the head is the first female. It is now a school largely run by females for both sexes, but the outlook of women conditions the nature of the school experience. I think the experience for boys is not always fully adequate. Boys need a fair sprinkling of male teachers to identify with in their actual lessons and in terms of discipline they need a type of text book which is not as pappy as they sometimes find. Boys are nationally behind girls in achievement at every age up to A' level.

Too Far

I think we have gone too far in terms of correcting the perceived rather than actual

The Milton Keynes-Oxford Coach keeps Buckingham's non motoring minority well connected, December 1999.

The White House undergoing renovation, March 1999.

vices of the past according to the moral standards of the present. Girls' attitudes are now much more confident, cocky even outrageous. They provoke staff. The first time I was aware of this was about fifteen years ago. I've never been so frightened in all my life because it was getting to the point where you couldn't touch students. When I first came, if I thought a student needed to be hit, I just did it one particular afternoon. I was teaching physics and a boy was fiddling with a gas tap. I whacked him with a ruler. I knew his father was a big burly chap. I thought he'd probably end my career when he came in to parents evening that same day. He came straight across, 'Put it there Mr Grimsdale, put it there! It's the greatest thing that's ever happened to Dennis, nobody's hurt him before. Well done. You're great!' Now at the end of my career I can reflect on that.

Great Gap

If I actually put my arm around a girl who was upset I'd be reported and that would be the end of my a career. There is that feeling now of a great gap between the male members of staff and the girls which can provoke an equal and opposite reaction because there are certain girls who will approach you provocatively just to see whether you'll go past the line. That makes it acutely difficult for young male staff. I realised this in the biology lab. Half way through the year a girl, I'll call Linda, joined the group. It was at the end of the lesson before lunch when I first met her. She came up to my desk, which was a sort of podium, and said, 'I need a text book sir.' 'That's fine,' I said. 'D'you like me?' she asked, thrusting her breasts toward my face. I was the only person with her in the room so hurriedly, I said 'Yes. I'll get you a text book.' 'Do you love me?' She asked, while opening several buttons on her blouse, making it clear she wore no bra. Since I was with her on my own I had no choice but to run for it. I never came back with the book. She was a girl boarder and went back to the boarding house where she made the same offer to a gas fitter working there. He took her up on it and so she did not return from lunch! I do feel sorry for young male staff, they are put to the ultimate test. Girls can terrorise them. Boys don't behave in as naughty a way as they used to, nor do they have the confidence they used to.

Ed Grimsdale

Railway Mess

It was a great mistake to close the railways. We always said, they've closed the branches that feed the main lines. People need cars to get to the main stations and spend a fortune clogging up the roads. They ran the railways down for years. We did a lot of make do and mend but it was better than today. There was a lot of cheap labour in the old days. The station master at Banbury wouldn't hold a main line train if a Buckingham train was late. Management and politicians didn't want it to work, that's why we've got the mess now.

Des Tunks

Stowe House around 1900 designed by Vanbrugh and Kent for Sir Richard Temple in the seventeenth century, it was over 900ft long with two wings.

Threatens

Milton Keynes threatens Buckingham businesses, it's only about ten minutes up the road. There are lots of strange businesses here now. The ladies' hairdressers at the White House would never have cottoned on if it wasn't for the middle management people who've moved here. There are a lot of little businesses on the estate behind Tesco, garages, workshops, small industrial units all expanding with the town. Even the cinema has become a town. I've gone to Ganderton's for years. There used to be a chamber of trade and I was invited to join for years. I finally did. It started at 7. 30 p.m. and was still droning on at 10 p.m. I decided it wasn't for me.

F.R. Markham

Miracle

Buckingham seems to miss its overlord – but the town has one major advantage; Milton Keynes. Some say the new city is a mega threat, but it is also a mega opportunity. I have always viewed Milton Keynes as a

Radclive Hall, the one time residence of Clive Birch MBE. (H.C.)

Nothing for youngsters to do? Well here's a nice little hobby increasingly popular with boy-racers hereabouts. This one lies abandoned off the A421 Ring Road, close to new developments facing toward Gawcott. (P.D.)

miracle ordained. Ordained because it sits slap in the centre of the county. Miracle because, of all the new towns it has worked in the first generation. It is a success visually, residentially, socially and commercially – of course it has its problems. The opportunity lies in its large and growing population, which seeks specialist services whether by shop or cafe or pub or individual experiences in museums, galleries or craft centres, concert venues and spectaculars at places like Stowe. Milton Keynes is Buckingham's marketplace, and almost certainly one of its major residential outposts – for not everyone wants to be seen to live in Milton Keynes, however otherwise attractive it may be. Buckingham has one other major advantage – its proximity to international motor and to Stowe's unique estate landscape, which offer twin hooks for the Buckingham experience – in an age which craves novelty, yet yearns for heritage.

Clive Birch MBE

Working On The Railway

I had some good mates working on the railway. when I moved to Claydon I thought I'd meet up with a lot of them, but I found most of them in the cemetery.

Des Tunks

They used to say Buckingham was behind the times but this Christmas it was ahead, proudly advertising 'Merry – or is it a fashionably dyslexic Mery? – Christmas 2001'.

Poetry Of A Town

I came to live in Buckingham
Twenty four years ago.
It was a close community,
The pace of life quite slow.
'You'll never be accepted'
I was told by everyone;
And then one day I was called
'My Duck' and thought perhaps I've won!

And so began my friendship
With the people of this town.
I became their local councillor;
And tried not to let them down.
And then in nineteen eighty six,
I'm so happy to declare,

I became a part of Buckingham;
As they kindly made me Mayor!

Much has happened since that
Date to the Buckingham I knew;
But thankfully its heritage
Is still alive and true.
The town has now developed
And grown considerably in size;
but it will always be my home,
my moving here was Wise!

I'll stand by them to this day!

Peggy Dale